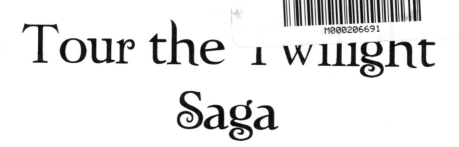

Tour the Twilight Saga

Book Two:

Vancouver, British Columbia

A Novel Holiday Travel Guidebook

By CD Miller

Tour the Twilight Saga Book Two:
Vancouver, British Columbia
A Novel Holiday Travel Guidebook

By CD Miller

Published by:
A Novel Holiday Travel Guidebooks
16614 226th Street
Ashland, NE 68003
http://www.anovelholiday.com

The publisher and author of *Tour the Twilight Saga* Book Two have taken great care to ensure that all information provided is correct and accurate at the time of manuscript submission. Unfortunately, errors and omissions—whether typographical, clerical or otherwise—sometimes occur. If you find an error or omission, please Email us and report it: chas@novelholiday.com

Changes in real-world site information will inevitably occur. As aptly stated by renowned travel guidebook author **Rick Steves**: "Guidebooks begin to yellow even before they're printed." For instance, the site-associated fees cited are those that were in effect during our last round of research and may be different when you visit.

Users of any *Tour the Twilight Saga* travel guidebook are advised to access the Internet links provided within each chapter in order to obtain the most up-to-date information during the planning of your Twilight Saga holiday.

The publisher and author(s) of *Tour the Twilight Saga* travel guidebooks hereby disclaim any liability to any party for loss, injury, or damage incurred as a direct or indirect consequence of errors, omissions, or post-manuscript-submission information changes, whether such errors, omissions, or changes result from negligence, accident, or any other cause.

Copyright © 2015 by Charly D Miller,
A Novel Holiday Travel Guidebooks Publishing Company
Printed in the United States of America
ISBN 978-1-938285-23-3

Publisher's Cataloging-in-Publication Data
Miller, Charly D, 1956 -
Tour the Twilight Saga Book Two: Vancouver, British Columbia
by Charly D Miller.
    p. cm.
        Includes index.
        ISBN 978-1-938285-23-3 (softbound) $29.95
        1. Travel Guides—United States—.
    I. Title.
F852.3 M460 2015

Table of Contents

Appendices

Tips for Twilighting in Canada

British Columbia Wildlife Warnings

Book Two Twi-Info

About This Book

Tour the Twilight Saga Book Two is designed to guide **Twilighters** (regular Twilight Saga fans) and **Twihards** (*die-hard* Twilight Saga devotees) to the Twilight Saga **film sites** found in and around **Vancouver, British Columbia, Canada**.

To visit the remarkable, real-world Twilight Saga **novel-related** locations found in the US state of Washington, see *Tour the Twilight Saga* **Book One—the Olympic Peninsula**.
http://tourthetwilightsaga.com/the-olympic-peninsula/

Twilight Saga Site Numbers

The numbers assigned to the fourteen (14) Twilight Saga sites identified in *Tour the Twilight Saga* (**TTTS**) Book Two are continued from the twenty-three (23) sites discussed in TTTS Book One. The order of their numbering is based on their location, as found if you were driving to them from Seattle, Washington. (Hey! We had to pick *some* order for numbering them, and alphabetically didn't seem helpful.)

Fee Examples

To give you an idea of what things might cost when you visit, we provided the site-associated fees that were in effect during our last round of research. Refer to the reference link provided to determine current fee expenses.

All fees cited in this book are provided in CANADIAN DOLLARS.

Use a free Internet currency converter—such as the one offered by **Oanda** (link below)—to obtain US Dollar or other foreign exchange rates, remembering that currency exchange rates change daily.
http://www.oanda.com/currency/converter/

Twilight Saga Site Rating Icons

Our *Tour the Twilight Saga* travel guidebook series is split into four books because, as of July 2015, we've discovered *eighty-seven* (87) Twilight Saga Sites in the world.

Not all of them are places even Twihards will want to visit.

During our research, we assessed each site critically and assigned it a rating based on our opinion of how **Twilicious** it is—how well what was described in the books, or seen on screen, can be recognized—and the number of interesting *non*-Twilight aspects and activities associated with the site.

Our **Great Site** icon indicates a Twilight Saga Site you don't want to miss.

Our **Might Be Fun** icon identifies places that are only moderately Twilicious, but offer tons of interesting *non*-Twilight aspects and activities. Each Might-Be-Fun Site chapter has an explanation of why it received that rating.

Our **Skip It** icon is assigned to places we feel are *not worth visiting*—even if you're a Twihard. The chapter explains why. We provide addresses or SatNav/GPS coordinates for Skip-It sites, but we don't offer directions for finding them. Twihards divinely inspired to visit a Skip-It site can investigate the location using information provided in the chapter.

Of the fourteen (14) Twilight Saga Sites found in and around Vancouver, BC:
- Four are Great Sites
- Six are rated Might Be Fun
  (Three of these are highly recommended!)
- Four are Skip It sites

The Twilighter Treaty

It is important that all Twilighters and Twihards be as polite as possible when visiting Twilight Saga sites, especially those situated on private property. It only takes *one* noisy or disrespectful fan to ruin the reception received by all Twilighters who visit thereafter. Please be the very best **Twilight Saga Ambassador** you can possibly be, and abide by the Twilighter Treaty everywhere you go.

The Twilighter Treaty:
**Do not trespass on private property.
Do not disturb—or photograph—the residents.
Do not bite any humans, for any reason.**

TwiTips, Twilight Saga Maps, and TwiLinks

To keep the size of our travel guidebook paperbacks from being too large to carry conveniently while **Twilighting** (touring Twilight Saga sites), we created several **TwiTips** PDFs (files containing extra **Twication**-planning information), **Twilight Saga Maps** to help you find your way around, and **TwiLinks** PDFs. All of these files are freely posted on our website:
http://tourthetwilightsaga.com/vancouver-british-columbia/book-two-twitips-maps/

The **Tips for Twilighting in Canada** appendix contains a directory of our TwiTips PDFs.

What are TwiLinks?

TwiLinks are PDFs containing the **reference website addresses** found within each Twilight Saga site chapter—as well as within the book's front matter and appendix. We created them for Twilighters who purchase a TTTS **paperback**, and for Twilighters who buy a TTTS **eBook**, but use an eReader from which Internet access isn't convenient.

After opening any TwiLinks PDF on your computer or tablet, you can simply *click on* each of the reference links, rather than having to type website addresses into your Internet browser.

Introduction

Why Vancouver, British Columbia?

When researching and writing her very first novel, Stephenie Meyer selected the little town of Forks—located in the Olympic Peninsula of the US state of Washington—as the primary setting for *Twilight*. Naturally, locations near to Forks soon crept into her manuscript: the Quileute Reservation, La Push First Beach, Port Angeles, and Seattle.

When plans began for filming *Twilight*, director Catherine Hardwicke hoped to shoot in the real-world novel settings. Unfortunately, Washington State's exorbitant filming fees at the time, and Forks' remote location, made shooting at these sites far too expensive for the meager budget allotted to the first Twilight Saga movie.

Areas in and around Vancouver, British Columbia were among the first scouted as potential film sites, but the US dollar had dropped below the Canadian dollar at that time—another blow to the budget. Thus, Hardwicke ended up filming *Twilight* in Oregon, and a few areas of southwestern Washington. (*Tour the Twilight* Saga Book Three)

Following the huge financial success of *Twilight* the movie, the state of Washington realized what it had missed out on and quickly enacted a new law, offering a 30 percent rebate of what a film company spends in the state during filming. At the same time, however the US/Canadian dollar exchange rate dramatically improved, and voila!—Vancouver became the hub for *New Moon*, *Eclipse*, and portions of *Breaking Dawn* Twilight Saga movie filming.

> "Even though the production team had loved shooting in Portland, ultimately it became more practical to stage principal photography in Vancouver, which over the years has built up the elaborate infrastructure vital to a movie production."

New Moon: The Official Illustrated Movie Companion, by Mark Cotta Vaz.

If you're interested, Wikipedia has four webpages that include fun facts regarding Twilight Saga filming that took place in and around Vancouver.
https://en.wikipedia.org/wiki/The_Twilight_Saga:_New_Moon
https://en.wikipedia.org/wiki/The_Twilight_Saga:_Eclipse
https://en.wikipedia.org/wiki/The_Twilight_Saga:_Breaking_Dawn_%E2%80%93_Part_1
https://en.wikipedia.org/wiki/The_Twilight_Saga:_Breaking_Dawn_%E2%80%93_Part_2

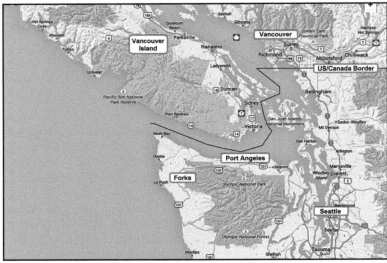

[Google Maps segments married & enhanced, ©2013 Google]

Where is Vancouver, British Columbia?

The province of British Columbia is found in the southwestern corner of Canada, immediately north of Washington State. As such, it is relatively easy to combine an Olympic Peninsula Twilight Saga novel location visit with a Twilight tour of Vancouver film sites.

Drive Times to Vancouver, BC from Twilight Saga Sites in Washington State:
- Seattle: 3 hours, 15 minutes
- Port Angeles: 4 hours, 45 minutes
- Forks: 4 hours, 45 minutes

About Vancouver, British Columbia

Vancouver is a massive, metropolitan area—the third-largest city in all of Canada. Nestled between the sparkling Northern Pacific Ocean and the majestic Coast Mountains, the city and its surrounding areas offer an amazing variety of activities and attractions.

> "Consistently ranked as one of the world's most livable cities, Vancouver lures visitors with its abundance of natural beauty, multicultural vitality, and cosmopolitan flair. The attraction is as much in the range of food choices ... as it is in the museums, shopping opportunities, and beaches, parks, and gardens.

[©2008 Shaund]

Indeed, the Vancouver package is a delicious juxtaposition of urban sophistication and on-your-doorstep wilderness adventure."

http://www.fodors.com/world/north-america/canada/british-columbia/vancouver

"Ringed by snow-capped, forested mountains dropping down to miles of sandy beaches, Vancouver is a city where you can snowboard and sail on the same day. ... Giant, colorfully carved totem poles tower above an impressive collection of First Nations masks and sculptures at the Museum of Anthropology. Visit the belugas, otters, and dolphins at the Vancouver Aquarium in Stanley Park, before seeing historic and modern art at the downtown Vancouver Art Gallery."

http://www.frommers.com/destinations/vancouver/690070

"Don't tell Montreal or Toronto but Vancouver is the culinary capital of Canada. Loosen your belt and dive right into North America's best Asian dining scene, from chatty Chinese restaurants to authentic *izakayas* (Japanese neighborhood pubs), or taste a rich smorgasbord of freshly caught seafood, including seasonal spot prawns and juicy wild salmon. The farm-to-table movement here has revitalized the notion of West Coast cuisine – anyone for succulent Fraser Valley duck and a side dish of foraged morels? And we haven't even started on about the craft-beer scene that has led the nation in recent years."

http://www.lonelyplanet.com/canada/vancouver

To learn more about Vancouver, visit any or all of the websites listed below. Be warned, however, you'll soon discover **the worst thing about Vancouver:** having to narrow down the number of things you want to do, based upon the limited amount of time you have to spend here!

http://wikitravel.org/en/Vancouver
http://vancouver.ca/
http://www.tourismvancouver.com/
http://www.hellobc.com/vancouver.aspx
http://www.vancouver-bc.com/

Lastly, be sure to read our **Tips for Twilighting in Canada** appendix. It contains a directory of the **TwiTips PDFs** we created to help you plan the most Twilicious possible Vancouver, BC Twication.

24

Keery Park

The Swan House Set Film Site for *New Moon* and All Subsequent Movies
The *New Moon* Edward-Bella Breakup Clearing Film Site

Google Maps & SatNav/GPS: 18731 28th Avenue, Surrey, BC V3S 9V2, Canada

Hours of Operation: This is a public park, open from dawn to dusk, 7 days a week.

Visit Time: Plan on 10 to 15 minutes for snapping empty park pix where the Swan House set once stood. Add up to 45 minutes (1 hour, total) to also find and photograph the Breakup Clearing.

The Swan House Set Film Site

[Twilight screenshot (enhanced)]

Exterior *Twilight* scenes of Charlie Swan's home were shot outside a real-world house located in a residential area of **St Helens, Oregon** (TTTS Book Three). Note the neighbor's home seen next to it on the left, and the open vista behind the house.

[New Moon screenshot (enhanced)]

For *New Moon* filming, a full-sized recreation of the St Helens house (empty inside) was constructed and installed in a little greenspace known as **Keery Park**, located in a rural area southeast of Vancouver, BC. Although three trees were installed to replicate those seen in the St Helens house front yard, other Swan House surroundings dramatically changed. Thanks to the magic of movies, however, few fans noticed the differences.

[©2013 Tara Miller, St Helens Swan House] [New Moon Special Features screenshot segment (enhanced)]

The only architectural difference between *Twilight* and *New Moon* Swan Houses was the addition of a **bay window** for Bella's bedroom, next to the chimney. To facilitate Jacob's demonstration of his newly developed wolfy athleticism, they also installed another large tree outside the bay window.

[Google Street View image segment (enhanced), ©2009 Google]

As it happens, the **Google Street View** car, with its panoramic camera snapping away, passed down 28th Avenue during *New Moon* filming! The images captured in 2009 no longer exist on Google Maps. But, you still can see some of them on an old **Letters to Twilight** blog.
http://letterstotwilight.wordpress.com/2009/10/07/do-you-see-uc-what-i-see/

[YouTube video screenshot segment (enhanced), ©2009 Amber Kaharuva]

Between *New Moon* and *Eclipse* filming, the Swan House set was covered with plastic and fenced in. Twilighter Amber Kaharuva visited during this time and posted a video of the site on YouTube.

"Warning: I have a Potty Mouth."
[She's not kidding.]

http://www.youtube.com/watch?v=6ealEChLv_4

After *Eclipse* shooting wrapped, the Swan House set was dismantled and moved to a warehouse. When needed for a few *Breaking Dawn* scenes in 2011, they pulled it out of storage and reassembled it on the same site.
http://www.surreyleader.com/entertainment/115222354.html

[YouTube video screenshot segment (enhanced), ©2011 Sarah Morrill]

During an extremely short window in March of 2011, when *Breaking Dawn* filming had finished but the Swan House set was still intact—and *uncovered*—three lucky Twilighters began their Vancouver Twilight Tour at Kerry Park. http://www.youtube.com/watch?v=JC6Wf7QQiSo

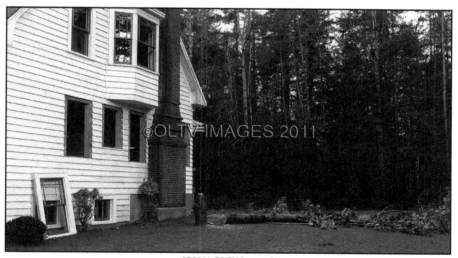

[©2011 OLTV Images]

On March 22nd, 2011, the Swan House set was dismantled for the last time—*maybe.*

> "Today the deconstruction began and it will never be built again.
> It took three weeks to build and a few days to take down. It will be

put in safe storage somewhere in the event that Stephenie Meyer ever finishes *Midnight Sun* and that book is made into a movie. Let's lobby Stephenie to finish the final book and make one more Twilight Saga Movie."

http://twidazzledgal.blogspot.com/2011/03/deconstruction-of-bella-swans-house-in.html

[©2013 CD Miller]

The Kerry Park Swan House Set site and nearby *New Moon* Breakup Clearing film site almost received a **Skip It** rating because there's absolutely nothing here to see, except for an empty—although, perfectly lovely—little park, and a brief forest trek. In the end, however, we assigned these side-by-side locations a **Might-Be-Fun** rating because:

- Kerry Park is easy to find.
- After sitting in a car for two hours, Twilighters driving from Seattle to Vancouver, BC will appreciate this opportunity to stretch their legs and breathe some fresh, piney-scented air. There are no toilet facilities here, but the route between Interstate 5 and Kerry Park is lined with plenty of gas stations and convenience stores. Make a potty stop after leaving the I-5 when heading to Keery Park.
- If the weather is nice and you have the time, following the forest path to the Breakup Clearing is a pleasant adventure.

The Breakup Clearing

[©2013 CD Miller]

The path that leads to the Breakup Clearing film site is just down the street from where the Swan House set was built. In the pic above, Chas' rental car is parked at the Swan House set site, and the path leading to the Breakup Clearing is seen at the left. Walk west from the park on the north side of 28th Avenue, watching on your right for the mouth of a forest path.

[©2013 CD Miller]

In 2013, a "Thanks for not Dumping Yard Waste" sign happened to be posted at the mouth of the forest path. Happily, if this unsightly sign is ever removed, the path is large enough to notice.

After walking only 85 steps down this path you'll arrive at a collection of small forest clearings.

[New Moon screenshot (enhanced)]

Look for the signature grouping of trees seen in the screenshot above. This is the fateful spot where Edward told Bella that the Cullen family was leaving Forks, and he was leaving *her*.

From the *New Moon* script:

Script Notes
Tears sting Bella's eyes. This can't be happening. He steps forward... kisses her forehead. She closes her eyes.
EDWARD
I promise, it will be like I never existed. Goodbye, Bella.

Script Notes
And here, for the first time, we see how truly agonizing this really is for Edward. But Bella doesn't see. By the time she opens her eyes - he's gone.

[©2013 CD Miller]

While Chas wasn't able to find the trees seen in the screenshot—her 2013 visit was rushed—this quiet, lushly picturesque area of forest is evocative of the scenes that were filmed here.

25

Gilleys Trail, Coquitlam
Jacob Black's House
http://www.coquitlam.ca/
http://en.wikipedia.org/wiki/Coquitlam
http://www.minnekhada.ca
http://en.wikipedia.org/wiki/Minnekhada_Regional_Park

Google Maps & SatNav/GPS: 1385 Gilleys Trail, Coquitlam, BC V3E 3H4
49.29694,-122.716761

Hours of Operation: This is a private residence.

Visit Time: 20 minutes to snap exterior pix.

Twilight Tongue Twisters:
- Coquitlam = "co-QUIT-lum"
- Minnekhada = "min-eh-KAH-dah"

[Breaking Dawn Part One screenshot (enhanced)]

Beginning with *New Moon,* all Twilight Saga scenes featuring the exterior of Jacob Black's house were filmed at this real-world location on **Gilleys Trail** road, northeast of Coquitlam.

[Eclipse Special Features screenshot segment (enhanced)]

When they first saw it, *New Moon* location scouts and director Chris Weitz fell in love with this property, its house and outbuildings—except for the buildings' paint color, which was green. According to the novel:

> "The Black's house was ... a small wooden place with narrow windows, the dull red paint making it resemble a tiny barn."

[New Moon Special Features screenshot segments (enhanced), above and below]

Happily, the homeowner allowed filmmakers to repaint everything red.

[©2013 CD Miller]

Happier still, the homeowner hasn't repainted since filming wrapped.

Jacob Black's House is a Private Residence

Please abide by the **Twilighter Treaty**, so that others can continue to enjoy this site long after you've gone.

Do not trespass. Stay on the street.
Do not disturb—or photograph—the residents.
Do not bite any humans, for any reason.

By the way; the **Wildlife Warnings** appendix at the back of this book is no joke! It isn't unusual to encounter **bears** while visiting *any* of the rural Twilight Saga sites, especially this one.

[Eclipse Special Features screenshot segment (enhanced)]

In fact, things became rather tense during *Eclipse* filming at Jacob Black's house, when the crew suddenly sighted a big black bear prowling the property's periphery. After a few minutes, the bear moved on, everyone breathed a sigh of relief and filming resumed.

Gilleys Trail—the road where Jacob Black's house is located—is the western boundary of **Minnekhada Regional Park.**
http://www.metrovancouver.org/services/parks_lscr/regionalparks/Pages/Minnekhada.aspx

Areas of this park are periodically *closed* when "bear activity is high." For example, this closure occurred in August of 2013:

> "Oliver Road CLOSED: Due to frequent and unpredictable bear activity, the section of Oliver Road within Minnekhada Regional Park is now closed to all park visitors, including pedestrians and cyclists. To protect people and bears, the area will be monitored and remain closed until further notice, most likely late October. While in the park, please follow safety signs, plan alternate routes and Be Bear Aware."

Oliver Road is the southern boundary of Minnekhada Regional Park. The south end of Gilleys Trail is *at* Oliver Road.

[©2014 Canadian Broadcasting Company]

In September of 2014, a school *in the city* of Port Coquitlam was locked down while conservation officers dealt with a large, lethargic black bear that was found napping in a nearby yard.

If you haven't already read our Wildlife Warnings, please do so before setting out on your Twilight Saga holiday.

Widgeon Slough Marsh

Motorcycle Lessons, a Stolen Kiss, a Broken Hand

http://twilightsaga.wikia.com/wiki/Filming_locations
http://www.spdf2013.com/program/Docs/ProtectionStewardship-Widgeon.pdf

Boathouse Google Maps & SatNav/GPS Coordinates: 49.348584,-122.647598

Hours of Operation: Dawn to dusk, weather permitting—this is a wilderness area

Visit Time: 4 to 5 hours

Twilight Tongue Twisters:

- Coquitlam = "co-QUIT-lum"
- DeBoville ="dih-BO-vill"
- Minnekhada = "min-eh-KAH-dah"
- Slough = "slew" (rhymes with grew)
- Widgeon = "WIDGE-un" (rhymes with bridge)

Widgeon Slough—aka **Widgeon Marsh Regional Park Reserve**—is a large freshwater tidal marsh located in a relatively undeveloped section of northeastern Coquitlam, British Columbia. Much of this land is ecologically sensitive wilderness, and public access is limited.

[Eclipse screenshot (enhanced)]

[*Battlestar Galactica* screenshot segment (enhanced)]

Due to its unique beauty, however, Widgeon Slough is no stranger to film and TV crews. **Planet Kobol** footage for *Battlestar Galactica* Season 1 and 2 episodes (2005) was shot in this same area.
http://www.imdb.com/title/tt0407362/

[New Moon screenshots (enhanced), above and below]

New Moon scenes of Jacob teaching Bella to ride a motorcycle were filmed in and around a Widgeon Slough boathouse and dock found at the SatNav/GPS coordinates provided above.

[Eclipse screenshot segment (enhanced)]

Also filmed at this site: *Eclipse* footage of Jacob and Bella on a walk—specifically, the dramatic scene in which he declares his feelings for her.

From the *Eclipse* script:

Jacob

I'm in love with you, Bella. And I want you to pick me instead of him. ... You wouldn't have to change for me. Or say goodbye to anyone. I can give you more than him. He probably can't even kiss you without hurting you. Feel that? Flesh and blood and warmth.

Jacob then steals an awkward kiss and Bella punches him in the face, breaking her hand.

[©2013 CD Miller]

☺Widgeon Slough is Assigned a Might-be-Fun Rating Because:

- A dirt road leading from Quarry Road to the Widgeon Slough film site is only 5.5 miles (8.6 km) from **Jacob Black's House** (Site #25), **but it is *not* open to the public.** BC Hydro and Power Authority (a Canadian electric utility) has an arrangement with the property owner to use this road for access—to what, we do not know. The sign is serious! If caught trespassing on the BC Hydro access road, you may be arrested. When Chas visited on a Monday afternoon in September of 2013, BC Hydro workers were present.
- **Twilighters who enjoy water sports, however, *can* visit this site via a rented canoe,** arriving at the dock seen on screen—which is open to the water-traveling public. (See directions below.) The little boathouse seen on screen also is still there.
- You'll need at least 3 hours to reach the site by canoe, snap some pix, and return to the rental boat landing. Even Twihards may consider this time expenditure excessive in relationship to the few screenshots that can be recreated here. If you can handle a canoe and have plenty of time, however, plan on scheduling 4 to 5 hours for this trek so that you can enjoy some of the many other wonders found at Widgeon Slough and Pitt Lake.

Please Note: Widgeon Slough is home to several rare and endangered species such as the green heron, western screech owl, red-legged frog, and the painted turtle. It is important that the habitat of Widgeon Slough birds and animals remain undisturbed by visitors.

Widgeon Slough woodlands also are often frequented by free-roaming wild **bears** and the occasional *cougar!* Be sure to read the **Wildlife Warnings** appendix at the back of this book before embarking on this trek.

If you come here—no matter how you arrive—please abide by

The *Wilderness* Twilighter Treaty

Leave No Trace of Your Passage.
Tread lightly and pack out all your trash.
Stay on the path or the road.
Do not trample any flora or foliage.
Do not disturb or *feed* the wildlife.
Do not photograph individuals encountered while visiting.
Do not bite any humans, for any reason.

A Substitute Motorcycle Lessons Site: DeBoville Slough
https://www.facebook.com/friendsofdebovilleslough

Trail Head SatNav/GPS Coordinates: 49.285429,-122.73379
A Nearby Address: 4062 Huber Drive, Coquitlam, BC V3E, Canada

Back when a few Vancouver tour companies were offering Twilight Saga film site tours, many fans wanted to visit the beautiful place where Jacob taught Bella to ride a motorcycle. Because Widgeon Slough is so difficult to access, however, a substitute site was selected, and Twilighters were (erroneously) told that the *New Moon* motorcycle lessons were shot on the **DeBoville Slough** trail.

[YouTube video screenshot (enhanced), ©2011 StarSightings]

If you watch the 2011 YouTube video (2.5 minutes) posted by Star Sightings, you'll see that the DeBoville Slough trail does look a lot like the Widgeon

Slough road where footage of Bella's maiden motorcycle drive was filmed. You'll not see the boathouse and dock, however, because DeBoville Slough is *not* the *New Moon* Motorcycle Lessons film site.
http://www.youtube.com/watch?v=qVrqOZ0Q8_I

Twilighters happy with an easily accessible—and somewhat similar—film site substitute can walk the DeBoville Slough trail by driving to the SatNav/GPS coordinates or address provided above. Just south of the Cedar Drive trail head is a little building containing public toilets, next to the small DeBoville Slough trail parking lot.

Plan on at least 2 hours to accomplish a leisurely 1 mile walk down the DeBoville Slough trail, snapping pix as you saunter, then back to your car.

[©2013 hostingbc.ca]

Canoeing to the *New Moon* & *Eclipse* Widgeon Slough Film Site

http://www.mapleridge-pittmeadows.com/things-to-do/adventure/canoeingkayaking/
http://www.bcadventure.com/adventure/explore/vancouver/fraser_valley/pitt.htm
http://www.vancouvertrails.com/trails/widgeon-falls/

Google Maps SatNav/GPS Coordinates: 49.348972,-122.615593
Address: Rannie Road, Pitt Meadows, BC V3Y 1Z1, Canada
(The address doesn't get you all the way to the canoe rental hut.)

To rent a canoe and paddle to this film site, book in advance by calling **Pitt Lake Canoe Rentals: 604-836-7117**. Their 25 canoes are offered on a first-come-first-serve basis.

The daytime canoe rental fee is $55, and includes life jackets, paddles, and bailing buckets—for water that *sloshes in* over the side; we're assured that the canoes do not leak!

Pitt Lake Canoe Rentals and boat landing is located at the north end of Rannie Road, on the east side of the **Pitt River**, at the southern border of **Pitt Lake**. The Widgeon Slough film site is approximately 1.3 miles (2.1 km) across the Pitt River, directly west of the Rannie Road boat landing, but **Siwash Island** lies *between* the two locations.

[Google Maps segments, married & enhanced, ©2013 Google]
http://www.TourTheTwilightSaga.com/WidgeonSloughCanoeTrek.pdf

In the **Widgeon Slough Canoe Trek** map we created and posted online:
- **A** is the Rannie Road canoe rental office and boat landing
- **B** is the Widgeon Slough dock and boathouse film site
- **C** identifies the mouth of **Widgeon Creek**

Tour the Twilight Saga authors are *not* water sports enthusiasts and we have not paddled here to recon the water route! Show our map to Pitt Lake Canoe Rental personnel and ask whether it is better to paddle around the *north* end of Siwash Island, or the *south* end of Siwash Island, to reach the film site. The answer may vary, depending on Pitt River and Widgeon Slough water conditions on the day of your visit.

> **Please Note:** We would deeply appreciate you posting an account of your Widgeon Slough canoe trek on the **Tour the Twilight Saga Facebook page** so that we can share it with other Twilighters.
> https://www.facebook.com/pages/Tour-The-Twilight-Saga/533851833326773

[Google Maps segment (enhanced), ©2013 Google]

Whether chancing arrest and arriving on foot, or safely sailing here in a canoe, your film site destination is the boathouse and dock seen in the background of *New Moon* screenshots found at the beginning of this chapter.

After snapping pix with the boathouse and dock in the background, turn around and head south (left) down the dirt road where Bella's maiden motorcycle drive was filmed. If you arrived via the publicly-accessible dock, BC Hydro won't consider you a trespasser, and you'll not be arrested!

As reported by tour guides who led fans to the faux film site at DeBoville Slough, filmmakers did, indeed, add a boulder at the curve of *this* road in order to film Bella's crash. They also used a stunt woman to perform Bella's accidental launch from the cycle and subsequent boulder collision. Jacob's ride to the rescue down this dirt road, however, was performed by Taylor Lautner—no stunt man needed.

After snapping pix on the road, return to the shore and wander around until you find the background seen in the *Eclipse* screenshots.

[©2013 pitt-lake.blogspot.com]

If you've allowed 4 to 5 hours for your trek, you can paddle up **Widgeon Creek** when finished at the film site, or go back around Siwash Island and head right to canoe into **Pitt Lake**. Several **ancient Katzie Indian pictographs** adorn the rock face that borders the western side of Pitt Lake.
http://pitt-lake.blogspot.com/2013/05/pictographs.html
http://www.katzie.ca/index.htm

[©2012 maplesunflower.wordpress.com]

Camping Twilighters can rent a canoe overnight ($85) and travel up Widgeon Creek to a free campsite. From there it's a short hike to the lovely Widgeon Falls. From all accounts, this is an experience not to be missed by those who enjoy camping.
http://www.vancouvertrails.com/trails/widgeon-falls/camping/
http://no-wrong-turns.blogspot.com/2014/04/widgeon-creek-by-kayaklions-and-tigers.html
http://alltrails.com/events/2014/03/short-notice-paddle-up-to-widgeon-slough-campsite-overnighter

Blue Mountain Park, Coquitlam
Film Site of Deleted *Eclipse* Scenes Following Bella's Graduation

Google Maps & SatNav/GPS: 49.253283,-122.865611
   Nearby Address: 578 Macintosh Street, Coquitlam, BC V3J 2C8, Canada

Hours of Operation: This is a public park.

Visit Time: 30 minutes to find and snap pix of a clearing surrounded by trees that *may* have been seen on screen.

[Eclipse screenshot (enhanced)]

The Forks High School class of 2006 graduation ceremony was filmed in the auditorium of **Como Lake Middle School** in Coquitlam.

[©2013 CD Miller]

Do not enter this school. If you do, you'll be violating the privacy of school children. Even if you manage to be *invited* into the auditorium, it looks nothing like what was seen on screen. Discovering the location of this school was only important to finding the nearby park, where deleted after-graduation scenes were shot—**Blue Mountain Park.**

[©2013 CD Miller]

Thanks to Van City Allie's blog spot and Google Street View, we know that the coordinates listed above identify the area where the *Eclipse* film crew was seen setting up for the deleted post-graduation scenes in 2009. Thus, the film site is somewhere within the trees near this location.

Alas, in 2015 we discovered that Van City Allie's blog spot was gone. So, we made a PDF of what we once found there.
http://www.TourTheTwilightSaga.com/B2/VanCityAllie2009.pdf

[Eclipse Special Features screenshot segments (enhanced) above and below]

The two screenshots above are the only clues available for finding the grouping of trees that identifies the film site.

☹ Blue Mountain Park in Coquitlam Earns a Skip-It Rating Because:

- If you come here, you'll be able to snap perfectly lovely trees-in-a-park pix. But, the likelihood of recognizing the actual film site is slim.
- Visiting this park requires a 30 minute out-of-the-way drive, another 30 minutes for finding and snapping some trees, and another 30 minutes to return to the route leading to your next location. These 90 minutes are far better spent enjoying sites that have more recognizable Twilight Saga photo-ops.

28

White Pine Beach, Sasamat Lake, Belcarra Regional Park

Riley & His Newborn Army Emerge from the Water

http://en.wikipedia.org/wiki/Belcarra_Regional_Park
http://en.wikipedia.org/wiki/Sasamat_Lake

Google Maps & SatNav/GPS: 49.322639,-122.88417

Hours of Operation: This public park is open from 8am to dusk throughout the year.

Visit Time: Schedule no less than 45 minutes here, *after* reaching the car park—which is a 1-hour round trip drive between the nearest Vancouver, BC Twilight Saga film sites.

ⓒ⑧⑳

[Eclipse screenshot (enhanced)]

In mid-September of 2009, the *Eclipse* B-unit crew spent two days shooting scenes of Riley and his Newborn army emerging from a body of water, while on their way to attack the Cullens. This footage was filmed at **White**

Pine Beach, on **Sasamat Lake**, in the Belcarra Regional Park—just north of Vancouver, BC.

[Eclipse Special Features screenshot segment (enhanced)]

A temporary metal dock was installed to accommodate cameras, sound and lighting equipment. Thanks to the Mandy's Mind blog, we have detailed information about the shoot.

> "It was amazing to see how many times they shot the same thing over and over and over, then re-set the camera angles and lights to re-shoot the same thing over and over again and again. Tedious and less glamorous than people think that's for sure."
>
> http://maliciousmandysmind.blogspot.com/2009/09/photos-from-this-weeks-set.html

Please Note: As of 2015, Mandy seems to have removed the pix from her older blog entries!

[Eclipse Special Features screenshot segment (enhanced)]

Mandy's Additional Observations:

- Scuba divers were on hand at all times to ensure cast safety.
- Each actor wore a wet suit beneath her/his costume—Sasamat Lake water is quite cold in the fall.
- Some vampires were dressed in business suits, others in trousers with hoodies or t-shirts.
- Each wore red contact lenses "that made their eyes look absolutely evil."
- White make-up was applied to their faces and visible upper body parts.

http://maliciousmandysmind.blogspot.com/2009/09/todays-filming-battle-scene-new-borns.html

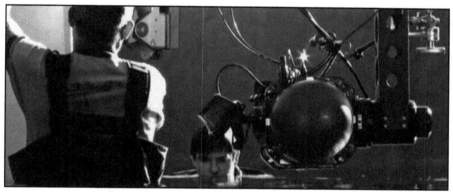

[Eclipse Special Features screenshot segment (enhanced)]

White Pine Beach is Assigned a Might-be-Fun Rating Because:

- Unlike footage seen in the *Eclipse* DVD Special Features segment, only snippets of Sasamat Lake background actually appear in the movie. There are no screenshot reproduction ops available here.
- This beach is such a popular spot for locals seeking to escape the summer heat that the road leading to White Pine Beach is often closed between 11am and 3pm on summer weekends, due to beach overcrowding and full car parks.
- The water of Sasamat Lake is wonderfully warm in the summer, but icy-cold during the spring and fall—requiring a wet suit if you intend to go swimming during the off-season.
- Although White Pine Beach's several car parks are only a 30 minute drive from Jacob Black's house in Coquitlam (**Site #25**), no less than

one hour should be allotted to accomplish a *round-trip* drive to this location between any Vancouver, BC Twilight Saga film sites.

- Surrounded by picturesque pine forest, Sasamat Lake and White Pine Beach are **absolutely *gorgeous***. Twilighters with an extra 2 (or more) hours of holiday time will thoroughly enjoy a trip to this site.

[©2007 (July) Lee A. Wood]

As previously mentioned, because Sasamat Lake's water is warm and wonderful for swimming in summer, White Pine Beach can be extremely crowded during those months.

[Internet-posted pic segment (enhanced), ©2013 (March) John Alexander Murphy]

We suggest that Twilighters visit in the spring or fall, when Sasamat Lake is icy-cold and White Pine Beach will probably be deserted. As you can see, this is a remarkably lovely place for relaxing and pretty pic snapping.

BTW: Please Read the Wildlife Warnings Appendix at the Back of this Book!

Belcarra Regional Park is a home to free-roaming black bears and possibly cougars.

🚗 Going to White Pine Beach, Sasamat Lake

Google Maps & SatNav/GPS: 49.322639,-122.88417

The coordinates we provide are for the point where you turn right to enter the loop drive that leads to all the White Pine Beach car parks.

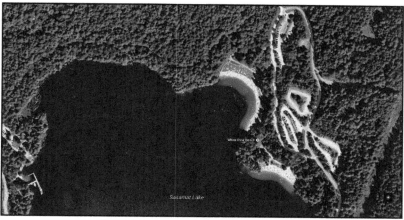

[Google Map segment (enhanced), ©2009 Google]

White Pine Beach is actually two beaches separated by a snippet of forest. *Eclipse* filming took place on the larger, northern beach.

[©2013 CD Miller]

Parking lot "F" is closest to the steps that lead to the northern beach (above, left), however all White Pine Beach parking lots afford easy access—wherever you park your car, it's only a 2 or 3 minute walk to the nearest beach entrance. Twilighters with mobility issues can access the southern beach via a paved ramp (above, right). From there, you can reach the northern beach by meandering down a level, well-maintained path which winds through a snippet of forest.

Happily, no steps lie between the southern beach ramp and any of the White Pine Beach parking lots. The car parks closest to the southern beach's ramp entrance, however, are "A" (the first one on your right when you arrive), and the lot requiring a handicap permit found at the end of the one-way drive that loops around and brings you back to where you started.

[©2013 Nancy Tinari]

Please Note:

- Both White Pine Beach areas have public toilets, but only the northern beach toilets (above) are unlocked during the off-season.
- The northern beach's concession stand is open only during the summer.
- Plenty of picnic benches are found in the grassy areas of both beaches.
- Dogs (and other animals) are not allowed on either beach.
- Alcohol consumption and cigarette smoking is strictly forbidden on both beaches.
- During the busy summer season, park wardens frequently patrol Sasamat Lake and its beaches. Random police checks occur at all times of the year, on the beaches as well as on Belcarra Park roads.
- No lifeguards are on duty at any time of the year. Thus, although both beaches have shallow-water areas safe for children to play in during the summer, White Pine Beach is strictly a swim-at-your-own risk area.

New Westminster
New Moon Film Sites:
The Paramount Theatre
~~One-Eyed Pete's Bar~~
Bella's Motorcycle Ride with a Stranger
Eclipse Film Sites:
Newborns Rampaging in Seattle
Volturi Viewpoint
http://www.newwestcity.ca/
http://en.wikipedia.org/wiki/New_Westminster

Google Maps & SatNav/GPS: 395 Columbia St, New Westminster, BC V3L, Canada (The New Westminster Downtown Parkade main entrance.)

Parkade Operation Hours: 24 hours a day, 7 days a week.

Film Site Operation Hours: All film sites are on public streets.

Visit Time: Schedule at least 2 hours here to spend 20 minutes at each film site.

Part of the Metro Vancouver area, **New Westminster** is located on the Burrard Peninsula, approximately 12 miles (19 kilometers) southeast of the City of Vancouver proper. Portions of its massive **Downtown Parkade**—aka the **Front Street Parkade**—are seen in scenes shot at four of the five New Westminster Twilight Saga film sites.

Unfortunately, part of this 1950s-era car park was destined for demolition in early 2015.
http://www.vancouversun.com/Westminster+demolish+Front+Street+parkade+year/10219201/story.html

The section slotted for removal stretches east from Begbie to Sixth Street, and its loss *would have* impacted the background of one film site, *if* that site were still there. (More about this below.) Happily, the Parkade portion that extends east of Sixth Street will remain intact, forever preserving two *Eclipse* film sites.

Additionally, the **Downtown Parkade** will remain a perfect place for Twilighter New Westminster Walk parking. Thus, the Google Maps/SatNav/ GPS address we provide at the beginning of this chapter (and below) will lead you to the main parkade entrance at Columbia and Fourth streets— **Point A** on the **New Westminster Walk** map included in the **Vancouver, BC Twilight Saga Maps PDF** freely posted on our website.

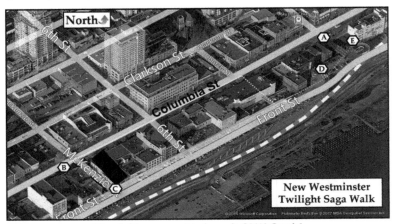

[Google Maps segment (enhanced), ©2013 Google]
http://www.TourTheTwilightSaga.com/B2/VBCtsMaps.pdf

The New Westminster Twilight Saga Walk Map Key

Solid Lines indicate travel on a surface with nothing but sky above.
Dotted Lines indicate travel beneath elevated structures, or within an enclosed walkway or building.

A: The New Westminster Downtown Parkade Main Entrance
395 Columbia St, New Westminster, BC V3L, Canada

B: The Paramount Theatre
652 Columbia Street, New Westminster, BC V3M 1A8, Canada

C: One Eyed Pete's Bar
49.202305,-122.908351

D: Seattle Newborn Rampage Film Site
409 Front Street, New Westminster, BC V3L 1A6, Canada

E: Volturi Viewpoint
(Above Point D)

Directions for walking between the New Westminster Points are provided within the film site explanations below.

📟Twilighters using public transportation, such as the **SkyTrain**, to travel within Metro Vancouver should disembark at the New Westminster **Columbia** station, located one block north of Point A. For more information, see our **Vancouver, BC Public Transportation Options** PDF:
http://www.TourTheTwilightSaga.com/TipsB2/B2PublicTransportation.pdf

🚶 Exit Columbia station on **Fourth Street** and turn right to walk south to **Columbia Street** (Point A). ♦ Turn right and walk east on Columbia Street for three blocks. ♦ Cross McKenzie Street, and look left for the Paramount Theatre (**Point B**).

CR8O

[©2013 CD Miller]

New Westminster Twilight Saga Walk Start—Point A
395 Columbia St, New Westminster, BC V3L, Canada

Columbia and Fourth streets—**Point A**—is the main entrance for the New Westminster Downtown Parkade. After driving up that ramp, you'll be on the top parkade level (**C deck**). ♦ Turn right and follow the signs that lead you down to the middle level (**B deck**). ♦ Once on the middle level, look for the roofed, **elevated walkway** that leads to the **Army & Navy** store.
http://www.armyandnavy.ca/

Park as near as you can to the elevated Army & Navy store walkway, stow valuables out of sight, and lock your car. ("Tarry for the Toot!") Write down your car's **license plate number** before leaving it—you'll need that to buy your car park ticket.

[©2013 CD Miller]

Wherever you park, a **pay station** will be nearby. You can use Canadian cash or any nation's major credit card to pay, and you'll not need to purchase more than **2 hours** of parking—*unless* you plan to do some antique shopping or catch a meal in the area. If that is the case, pay for at least **3 hours**.

🚶 Directions from the Lower Parkade Level to Point B

Walk through the elevated walkway into the Army & Navy store. ♦ Go through the store and exit via the main entrance on Columbia Street. ♦ Turn left and walk two blocks southeast. ♦ Cross McKenzie Street. The **Paramount Theatre** will be on your left.

[New Moon screenshot (enhanced)]

[©2013 CD Miller]

The Paramount Theatre (Point B)
652 Columbia Street, New Westminster, BC V3M 1A8, Canada

Exterior *New Moon* footage of Bella and Jessica's Port Angeles trip to see *The Dead Come Back*—a fictional zombie movie—was shot outside the real-world **Paramount Theatre** on Columbia Street in New Westminster. In addition to snapping pix of the Paramount's iconic marquee (above), below is a screenshot you can recreate when visiting.

[New Moon screenshot (enhanced)]

The scalloped light frames seen above Bella and Jessica are still there, as is the ticket window seen below.

[New Moon screenshots (enhanced) above and below]

Exterior footage of Bella's *New Moon* trip to Port Angeles with Jacob and Mike to watch *Face Punch* (another fictional film) was also shot here.

The southeast corner of Columbia and McKenzie Street is seen in the background of the screenshot above. Unfortunately, the old **Copp's Shoes** shop—built after the Great Fire of 1898—closed in 2012 and was replaced by a bridal shop. Worse than that, the entire building was destroyed by fire in October of 2013.

Copp's Shoe Store Rose from Ashes—Perishes in Flames

http://www.royalcityrecord.com/news/new-westminster-s-copps-shoe-store-rose-from-ashes-perishes-in-flames-1.656232

Paramount Theatre History

The Paramount Theatre occupies a building erected in 1899. In 1903, the **Edison Theatre** began operating here, featuring live Vaudeville acts.

Sometime in the early 1940s, the Edison started occasionally showing "moving-pictures." In 1948, the theatre was leased to **Paramount-Famous Players** and became a dedicated motion picture theatre. Many interior and exterior renovations occurred at this time, including the installation of a large neon marquee proclaiming its new name—**The Paramount Theatre**.

Unfortunately, when New Westminster's downtown business area deteriorated in the mid-80s, the Paramount movie theatre was closed. The building remained vacant until 1993, when it was reopened as the **Paramount Gentlemen's Club**—a non-alcoholic, adult entertainment theatre. As of November 2014, the Paramount remains open, as a **strip club**.
http://www.paramountgirls.com/

Despite the business currently in operation here, this building was formally recognized as one of **Canada's Historic Places** in 2004, because it is among the oldest surviving motion picture theatres in British Columbia.

> "The Paramount Theatre was highly significant to the community, as television was not yet widely available and movies were the main form of public entertainment."
>
> http://www.historicplaces.ca/en/rep-reg/place-lieu.aspx?id=3413

No Twilight Saga movie footage was filmed *inside* the Paramount Theatre.

Interior *Face Punch* lobby scenes were shot in Vancouver's **Ridge Theatre** (see the Inaccessible Vancouver, BC, Film Sites chapter). Thus, unless you're a Twilighter interested in enjoying the … amenities … offered at a Canadian strip club, you need not enter the Paramount Theater.

🚶 Directions from Point B to Point C

Return to the intersection of Columbia and McKenzie streets. ◆ Turn right and look southeast on McKenzie street toward the riverfront.

One Eyed Pete's Bar Film Site (Point C)
49.202305,-122.908351

The very first time Bella experienced a vision of Edward reminding her that she'd promised not to do anything reckless occurred as she walked down

McKenzie Street toward a group of dangerous-looking dudes perched on motorcycles parked outside **One Eyed Pete's** bar.

One Eyed Pete's is an entirely fictional bar—it doesn't exist anywhere in the real-world, including here. Filmmakers created the illusion of One Eyed Pete's bar by hanging a couple wall posters on a real-world building, and installing a neon bar sign at its corner. Thanks to lighting effects, the bar's main entrance *seems* to be around the corner, on Front Street, but it's never actually seen on screen. Can we say cheap film set? I think we can. But, it worked!

New Moon screenshot (enhanced)]

[©2013 CD Miller]

When CD Miller visited on September 17th, 2013, the view down McKenzie Street from Columbia Street looked exactly as it did when the One Eyed Pete's scenes were filmed here in 2009. Although worried that demolition of the parkade's west-end would ruin the background aspect of this screenshot's recreation opportunity, Miller remained happy that snapping at least the building's corner could still be accomplished. Unfortunately, 23 days later, **a fire destroyed the entire building!**

[©2013 Nick Procaylo, PNG]

http://www.vancouversun.com/Westminster+building+destroyed+massive+fire+will+rebuilt/9028923/story.html

[©2014 Dan Burritt/CBC]

A year after the fire, the west end of the parkade was still there (demolition isn't slated to start until February, 2015), but only a vacant lot now exists where One Eyed Pete's building once stood.
http://www.cbc.ca/news/canada/british-columbia/new-westminster-fire-then-and-now-1.2794734

We continue to include identification of this lost film site so that visiting Twilighters can pause before heading to the next New Westminster film site, and take a moment to morn the loss of One Eyed Pete's bar.

🚶 Directions to where Bella's Motorcycle Ride with a Stranger was Filmed—aka Directions from Point C to Point D Part One

Walk to the south end of McKenzie Street (Point C—the corner where One Eyed Pete's bar was filmed in 2009), and turn left on Front Street. You're there!

ᚳ₰ᚸ

[New Moon screenshot (enhanced)]

Footage of Bella riding on the back of a stranger's motorcycle—who's name, according to the script, was **Chet**—was shot on Front Street as they drove northeast from McKenzie Street, next to the Downtown Parkade section that stretched between McKenzie and Sixth streets, in 2009.

Although the 2015 west-end parkade demolition project will destroy the parkade portions seen during the motorcycle ride scenes between Begbie and Sixth Street, at least one of the following Bella Motorcycle Ride screenshots should remain reproducible.

The first screenshot below was filmed from Bella and Chet's point of view as they approached the Front Street intersection with Sixth Street. **Interesting Note:** Chet was driving east-bound in what was then a *west-bound* traffic lane. Movie Magic.

[New Moon screenshots (enhanced) above and below]

The screenshot above was filmed *from* the Sixth Street intersection, looking back west down Front Street toward McKenzie Street and One Eyed Pete's bar. After this section of parkade is demolished, the pillars seen above will be gone, but the storefronts will still be present.

[©2013 CD Miller]

By The Way: There are many marvelous shops on Front Street, between McKenzie Street (Point C) and the next film site (Point D)—shops that will still be here after parkade demolition. Above is the **Antique Alley Antique Collectables and Movie Props** store. Although they don't offer *Twilight* movie props, there are plenty of interesting things here.
http://antiquealleymovieprops.com/

🚶 Directions from Point C to Point D Part Two

After snapping pix of the Bella motorcycle ride screenshots above, resume walking northeast on the Front Street sidewalk next to the elevated Downtown Parkade section *not* scheduled for demolition. ♦ When the parkade angles northeast and you begin walking *beneath* it, look to your left. ♦ The last lot on the left, below the parkade's east end, is Point D on the New Westminster Walk Map.

[©2012 Google Street View segment (enhanced)]

Newborn Rampage Film Site (Point D)
409 Front Street, New Westminster, BC V3L 1A6, Canada

On two nights in August of 2009, this gnarly-looking, New Westminster private parking lot was transformed into a **Seattle back street** set.

[*Eclipse* film site set photo segments, above and below, ©2009 Mandy]
http://maliciousmandysmind.blogspot.com/2009/08/revisiting-last-nights-set-putting.html

Thanks to photos snapped here by Mandy on the morning after *Eclipse* filming, we can see that several rusty-looking façades were added to this site. Obviously, all *Eclipse* set dressings are long gone and the lot has been cleaned up. Furthermore, the door seen behind the overturned car in the screenshot below has since been garishly painted to welcome **New Dawn Doggie Daycare** patrons. Happily, you'll recognize *some* of the structural elements seen on screen at this site.

[©2013 CD Miller]

[Eclipse Special Features screenshot segment (enhanced)]

From the *Eclipse* script:

EXTERIOR SEATTLE—ISOLATED STREET—NIGHT

Riley, exasperated, stands next to a late model sedan that lies upside down in the dark street. Smoke comes from the engine, a fire ignites. Inside the car, a woman screams—

RILEY: What did I say about keeping a low profile?!

[Eclipse Special Features screenshot (enhanced)]

From the *Eclipse* script:

CAMERA CRANES UP AND BACK TO AN OVERPASS IN THE DISTANCE

—where we find four people, utterly motionless, looking down at the mayhem.

PUSH IN to find that they're the VOLTURI.

Point E is a film site located on the circular section of a ramp that leads up from the east end of the New Westminster Downtown Parkade's middle level (B deck) to the top level (C deck). If you parked on the B deck, you'll drive up this ramp when leaving the car park and heading to your next Twilight Saga destination.

As seen in the screenshot below, Point E is visible from—and was *filmed* from—the Seattle rampage set on Front Street. Thus, the best Point E screenshot recreation opportunity is found at Point D.

[Eclipse Special Features screenshot segment (enhanced)]

[©2013 CD Miller]

If there are several people in your party, send the others up to pose at the Volturi viewpoint before taking your pix.

🚶 Directions to Point E from Point D

After snapping pix at the Seattle rampage film site, head to the east end parkade stairs (seen in the photo above) and go up to the B deck parking level. ◆ Turn left and you'll see the Point E film site.

♿ Note for Those in Wheel Chairs or Unable to Climb Stairs

After snapping pix at the Seattle rampage lot, head back the way you came, watching on your right for the Front Street entrance to the **Army & Navy** department store's basement. ◆ Go in and take the elevator up one floor to the ground level (Columbia Street level), and return to the lower parkade level via the roofed, elevated walkway. ◆ Turn left and you'll see the Point E film site at the east end.

[©2013 CD Miller]

Volturi Viewpoint (Point E)

The Special Features screenshot seen below can be recreated by standing at the pole by the up-ramp's entrance, and staying safely out of the traffic lane.

[Eclipse Special Features screenshot (enhanced)]

[©2013 CD Miller]

Twihards divinely inspired to risk being **struck by a car careening up the ramp** to snap pix *from* the actual Volturi viewpoint will be disappointed. The Seattle Newborn Rampage site no longer looks anything like the few shots filmed from Point E.

[Eclipse Special Features screenshot (enhanced)]

There is no upside-down car in the lot, the rusty façades masking a lower wall and the building that looms on the right are long gone.

When finished at Point E, you're done with the New Westminster Twilight Saga Walk! Return to your car and head to your next location.

🚊 Directions for Twilighters who journeyed here on the SkyTrain

🚶 Go up the stairs to the top Parkade level (C deck) and turn left.

[©2013 CD Miller]

Walk north on the west side of Fourth Street (seen above, at center), watching on your left for the New Westminster Columbia station.

30

David Thompson Secondary School
Forks High School Cafeteria Scenes seen in *New Moon* and *Eclipse*
★Bonus Info: The *New Moon* Forks High School Parking Lot Film Site
http://go.vsb.bc.ca/schools/thompson
https://www.facebook.com/pages/David-Thompson-Secondary-School/112093688802495

Google Maps & SatNav/GPS: 1755 E 55th Avenue, Vancouver, BC V5P, Canada

Hours of Operation: This is a public high school. It isn't open to *strangers*. Do not enter it!

Visit Time: Little more than 5 minutes is required to snap exterior pix here that look absolutely nothing like anything seen on screen.

(380)

[Google Street View image segment (enhanced), ©2011 Google]

David Thompson Secondary School—aka High School (Canada)—is attended by children in the 8th through 12th grades. In April of 2009, the school's cafeteria became the **Forks High School** cafeteria for *New Moon* filming. Four months later, *Eclipse* Forks High School cafeteria footage was shot here.

☹ The David Thompson School Earns a Skip-It Rating Because:

- If you enter this school you'll be violating the privacy of school children. Please abide by the **Twilighter Treaty** and stay out!
- Even if you manage to be *invited* into the school's cafeteria, it looks nothing like what was seen on screen—as we'll demonstrate below.
- We included this film site only to be thorough in our presentation of places where Twilight Saga filming took place. Your Vancouver Twilight tour time will be far better spent enjoying sites that offer Twilight Saga photo-ops.

[New Moon screenshot (enhanced)]

The only Forks High School cafeteria elements that exist in the real-world David Thompson cafeteria are the blinds on the windows, the round tables, the steel and plastic chairs. **That's it.**

[Eclipse film site photo segment (enhanced) ©2009 TwiFans.com]

For both *New Moon* and *Eclipse* scenes, a lane of trees was erected in the staff car park next to the cafeteria, and the windows were draped with multi-national flags for *Eclipse* filming. Obviously, these trees and flags aren't there anymore.

[Eclipse Special Features screenshot segment (enhanced)]

Again, even if you manage to be invited into the cafeteria, it looks nothing like what was seen on screen.

In the interest of full disclosure, we reluctantly admit that a few *New Moon* Forks High School **hallway** scenes also were shot inside David Thompson school.

[New Moon screenshot segments (enhanced), above and below]

Although you may be able to recognize where these scenes were shot, it is *unacceptable* to trespass within this school. **Please do not do so!**

[Twilight screenshot segment (enhanced)]

*The *New Moon* Forks High School Exterior Film Site Bonus Info

When filming *Twilight*, director *Catherine Hardwicke* shot all exterior Forks High School footage outside **Kalama High School** in Kalama, Washington, USA (TTTS Book Three). Because *New Moon* filming took place almost entirely in and around Vancouver, BC—the only exception being scenes shot in **Italy** (TTTS Book Four)—director Chris Weitz employed movie magic to film Forks High School parking lot scenes for *New Moon*.

Weitz had set designers recreate the exterior Kalama High School **steps** and **railings**, as well as their associated **concrete planters** and **shrubs**. In September of 2009, those set pieces were installed within **an empty car park** somewhere in the Vancouver, BC area, with giant green screens erected behind them. In post-production, the green screens were replaced with computer-generated-images of the real-world Kalama High School building. V*oilà*! Forks High School parking lot in Vancouver.

[New Moon Special Features screenshot segments (enhanced), above and below]

Alas, we failed to discover the location of this Vancouver parking lot. Had we found it, however, the film site would merely be a large, empty car park that looks nothing like Forks High School's parking lot. So, we don't feel too badly about not finding it.

There You Have It.

Do not bother looking for *any* aspect of Forks High School in the Vancouver, BC area. It's not there. Your Vancouver holiday time is much better spent visiting the many Twilight Saga film sites that are recognizable—and *accessible!*

Gastown & Downtown Vancouver

Four *Eclipse* Film Sites:
　Riley Leaving The Pike Pub (in "Seattle")
　Victoria's Initial Attack on Riley
　Rosalie's Rochester Assault Flashback
　Rosalie's Revenge Flashback
A *Breaking Dawn* Part 1 Film Site:
　Edward's Movie Theatre Flashback
A *Breaking Dawn* Part 2 Film Site:
　Bella Parking Before Meeting J Jenks

http://en.wikipedia.org/wiki/Gastown
http://www.gastown.org/
http://vancouver.about.com/od/walkingtours/tp/Vancouver-Gastown-Shopping-Guide.htm
http://www.seegastown.com/

Google Maps & SatNav/GPS: 160 Water Street, Vancouver, British Columbia V6B 2K8 (That is the most convenient car park address. Public transportation options are discussed below, in the **Going To Gastown** section.)

Car Park Operation Hours: 24 hours a day, 7 days a week.

Film Site Operation Hours: All but Edward's movie theatre and Rosalie's revenge film sites are places on public streets, accessible 24/7.

Visit Time: Merely the roundtrip walk between our preferred car park and the six film sites requires approximately 1 hour. Schedule *at least* 2½ hours here to spend 20 minutes at each site before having to dash to the next one. Realistically, a Gastown Twilight Saga Walk will take about 3½ hours to accomplish. If you're interested in exploring any of the many marvelous non-Twilight sights encountered along the way, schedule at least 4½ hours for your visit.

[The Gastown Steam Clock, ©2010 Joan Felip]

Gastown is a national historic site situated in the northeast corner of Vancouver's downtown area and is considered the city's birthplace.

When Canada became a nation in July of 1867, the Burrard Inlet's south shore was a wilderness inhabited by only one non-native element: a lumber mill, whose owner banned alcohol from the premises. In September of that year, a Yorkshire steamship captain called "Gassy Jack" Deighton (a nickname derived from his penchant for spinning tall tales) arrived, bearing a single barrel of whiskey. He told the mill workers that if they'd build him a saloon, he'd serve them drinks. One day later, Gassy Jack's Saloon was up and running barely a stone's throw away from the mill, and thus was born what quickly became known as Gastown.

As more and more white settlers and business entrepreneurs arrived, Gastown flourished and grew. Nineteen years later, in April of 1886, Gastown was officially incorporated as the **City of Vancouver**.

During the Great Depression era (1930s-40s), Gastown gradually deteriorated into a stereotypical skid row area. When threatened with demolition in the 1960s, however, a group of concerned citizens campaigned to save its historic architecture and preserve its distinctive character. Other Vancouverites rallied behind them, and not only was Gastown saved, it was *reborn*.

In 1971, the provincial government of British Columbia declared Gastown an historic area, and in 2009 it was officially designated a National Historic Site of Canada. Thus, Gastown will forever be protected and preserved.

Downtown Vancouver offers a multitude of marvelous non-Twilight landmarks and tourist attractions. If you'll have time for more than our Gastown Twilight Saga Walk, be sure to explore other Vancouver travel guidebooks and websites when planning your trip. For instance, take a look at the three Vancouver Walking Tours featured on *Frommers'* website.

Walking Tour 1: Downtown & the West End
Start: The Fairmont Hotel Vancouver.
Finish: Cathedral Place.
http://www.frommers.com/destinations/vancouver/690123#sthash.HUADmGiH.dpbs

Walking Tour 2: Gastown & Chinatown
Start: Canada Place.
Finish: Maple Tree Square.
http://www.frommers.com/destinations/vancouver/690124#sthash.eEa0pzVr.dpbs

Walking Tour 3: Yaletown, Granville Island & Kitsilano
Start: The Vancouver Public Library at Homer and Georgia Streets.
Finish: The Capers Building, 2285 W. 4th Ave. (at Vine St.), in Kitsilano.
http://www.frommers.com/destinations/vancouver/690125#sthash.pRInvFTG.dpbs

The Twilight Saga Film Sites
Only the first two film sites in this chapter are actually *in* **Gastown**. The four others are nearby, within the **Downtown Vancouver** area. To minimize confusion, we're simply referring to the entire area as the Twilight Saga Gastown area.

To help you swiftly and efficiently visit each of these sites, we created a **Gastown Twilight Saga Walk Map**, which you'll find in the **Vancouver, BC Twilight Saga Maps PDF** freely posted on our website.

Gastown
Twilight Saga Walk

[Google Maps segments married & enhanced, ©2013 Google]
http://www.TourTheTwilightSaga.com/B2/VBCtsMaps.pdf

The Gastown Twilight Saga Walk Map Key

Solid Orange Lines indicate the walk route for Twilighters who drive to the area.

Dotted Orange Lines indicate walk routes for Twilighters using public transportation to follow before and after the walk route for driving Twilighters.

Solid Yellow Lines indicate the non-Twilight Gastown landmarks walk route for driving Twilighters.

WS: Waterfront Station
Located on West Cordova Street, near the Seymour Street intersection. Serving Expo, Millennium, and Canada Lines

SC: The Gastown Steam Clock
49.284444, -123.108889

P: The two Gastown EasyPark buildings

A: The Water Street Easy Park Car & Pedestrian Entrance/Exit
160 Water Street, Vancouver, BC V6B 2K8

GJ: Gassy Jack's Statue in Maple Tree Square, and Gaoler's Mews

BAS: Blood Alley Square

B: Lamplighter Pub Patio Film Site
49.283718, -123.106414—or 212 Abbott St, Vancouver, BC V6B 1B2

C: Trounce Alley Film Site
49.283424, -123.106567—or 247 Abbott St, Vancouver, BC V6B 2K8

D: Beatty Street Film Site
538 Beatty Street, Vancouver, BC V6B 1S5

E: The Orpheum Theatre Peek-Inside Point
49.279868, -123.120235—near 601 Smithe Street, Vancouver, BC V6B 1L7

F: The Orpheum Theatre Marquee & Star Walk
884 Granville Street, Vancouver, BC V6Z 1K3

G: Hornby Street Film Site
49.283596,-123.12035—or 700 Hornby St, Vancouver, BC V6E

H: The Fairmont Hotel Vancouver
900 West Georgia Street, Vancouver, BC, V6C 2W6

CCS: Vancouver City Centre Station
Entrance at West Georgia Street & Granville.
Serving the Canada Line.

GS: Granville Station
Located between West Georgia Street and Dunsmuir Street,
with entrances from Granville Street and Seymour Street.
Serving Expo and Millennium Lines.

I: The West Cordova Street Easy Park Car & Pedestrian Entrance/Exit
240 West Cordova Street, Vancouver, BC V6B 2N3

Directions for walking between all Gastown Twilight Saga Walk Points are provided within the film site information sections below.

Going To Gastown
🚊 Gastown Twilight Saga Walk via Public Transportation

Twilighters using public transportation—such as the **SkyTrain**—to travel within Vancouver should arrive via the Waterfront Station (**WS** on the Gastown Twilight Saga Walk Map). When finished with your Gastown Twilight Saga Walk, you can depart via the Vancouver City Centre Station (**CCS**), the Granville Station (**GS**), or walk back to the Waterfront Station.

For more information, see our **Vancouver, BC Public Transportation Options** PDF:
http://www.TourTheTwilightSaga.com/TipsB2/B2PublicTransportation.pdf

Directions from WS to SC and Point A

Exit the Waterfront Station on West Cordova Street. ♦ Turn left and walk southeast to the intersection of Richards Street and Water Street. ♦ Turn left and walk southeast on Water Street for one block, where you'll find the Gastown Steam Clock (**SC**) at the intersection of Cambie Street. ♦ Continue southeast on Water Street for a half block to reach the Easy Park entrance (**Point A**). ♦ From there, follow directions found below.

http://www.TourTheTwilightSaga.com/B2/VBCtsMaps.pdf

 Consider Riding the Vancouver Hop-On/Hop-Off Busses and Trolley

Whether driving or using public transportation to reach Gastown, you may enjoy riding the Vancouver Hop-On/Hop-Off busses or Trolley while visiting this area. Convenient and scenic, these guided tours can be fun. Our **Vancouver, BC Twilight Saga Maps PDF** includes maps made from sections of the Hop-On/Hop-Off bus and Trolley routes, with our Gastown and Downtown Vancouver Twilight Saga Site identifiers added—as well as the identifiers for Twilicious places-of-interest found in nearby **Stanley Park** (Site #32).

https://westcoastsightseeing.com/hop-on-hop-off/
http://www.vancouvertrolley.com/tours/hop-on-hop-off

ભૂષ્ઠ

🚗 Gastown Twilight Saga Walk via Automobile

For Twilighters driving to Gastown, our preferred Easy Park facility is a huge, multi-level parkade with 1418 stalls, where you'll find a convenient parking space. This car park occupies two buildings situated between two one-way streets, with elevated ramps spanning the alley between them.

http://www.easypark.ca/easypark-lots/locations-and-rates/Gastown-Parking-Vancouver-Lot-31.aspx?lang=-123.1072&lat=49.284

If approaching Gastown from the east, use the Water Street entrance (**Point A**). 160 Water Street, Vancouver, BC V6B 2K8

If approaching from the west, use the West Cordova Street entrance (**Point I**). 240 West Cordova Street, Vancouver, BC V6B 2N3

Park *anywhere* within this two-building facility.

If you follow our map, you'll start your trek by exiting at the Water Street pedestrian exit, and end it by using the West Cordova Street pedestrian entrance. Thus, the walking distance for our Gastown Twilight Saga tour is relatively the same no matter where you park.

You can park and pay on exit at anytime of the day or night. Or, you can park and purchase a specific amount of parking time at the nearest pay station. Those who pre-pay for parking can use their pay station receipt to exit via an express lane.

Be sure to note the level and space number wherever you park, and follow the safety directions liberally posted throughout this facility.

[©2013 CD Miller]

Yes! The Vancouver Parking Authority places "bait cars" in popular car parks to dissuade thieves from breaking into parked vehicles. If you fail to follow the posted Prevent Theft tips, thieves may mistake your car for a bait car, and leave it alone. It is a far better idea, however, to minimize the motivation for a break-in by *following* the posted Prevent Theft tips.

- Move ALL contents—whether or not they are "valuables"—from your car's interior to the trunk (boot).
- Open the glove box, ashtray, and center console, demonstrating that all are *empty*.
- Make sure there is *nothing* on the car's rear seat—this will allow you to *skip* the "Fold down back rear seat" tip.
- Lock the Car—or, as we put it, "Tarry for the Toot!" (Push the key's lock button until the horn honks, confirming that the car is locked.)

After parking, follow signs leading to the **Water Street Pedestrian Exit**, Point A on the Gastown Twilight Saga Map.

Walking Directions from Point A to Point B for Driving Twilighters

To assist driving Twilighters interested in visiting non-Twilight-Saga Gastown landmarks—something we highly recommend—we provide two sets of walking directions between Points A and B. The solid yellow lines on our Gastown Twilight Saga Walk Map represent the **Gastown Landmarks** route. The solid orange lines represent the **Film-Sites-Only** route.

🚶 Points A to B Gastown Landmarks Walking Directions

- Exit the Gastown Easy Park on the south side of Water Street (**Point A**).
- Turn left and walk half-a-block northwest on the **south side** of Water Street to Cambie Street. Look to your right (north) and you'll see the Gastown Steam Clock (**SC**) on the northwest corner of this intersection.
  http://en.wikipedia.org/wiki/Steam_clock#Gastown_steam_clock
  http://www.gastown.org/live-work/item/8688-the-return-of-the-steam-clock

- When finished, cross to the north side of Water Street and head back the way you came (southeast), enjoying the galleries and shops found on Water Street's **north side** as you go.
- When you reach Carrall Street, look to your right for Maple Tree Square and the statue of Gassy Jack (**GJ**). The entrance to **Gaoler's Mews** is behind Gassy's statue.
  http://www.lonelyplanet.com/canada/vancouver/sights/squares-plazas/maple-tree-square
  http://www.venturevancouver.com/gassy-jack-statue-gastown-vancouver
  http://www.ghostsofvancouver.com/gaolers_mews.htm

- When finished, walk a few steps southwest to the Carrall Street Trounce Alley entrance and turn right.
- Walk a short distance west, watching on your left for Blood Alley Square (**BAS**). Info about Blood Alley Square is in the Point C section of this chapter.
- When finished in Blood Alley Square, you *could* continue west in Trounce Alley to **Point C** on the Gastown Twilight Saga Walk Map. But, we suggest that you go back out the way you came, turn left at Carrall Street, and return to Water Street. There, you can turn left to walk northwest for one block, enjoying Water Street's **south side** galleries and shops as you go.
- At Abbott Street, turn left and you'll be at **Point B**: The Lamplighter Pub's patio doors.

🚶 Points A to B Twilight-Saga Film Sites *ONLY* Directions

- Exit the Gastown Easy Park on Water Street (**Point A**).
- Turn right and walk half-a-block southeast along the south side of Water Street to Abbott Street.
- Cross to the east side of Abbott Street
- Turn right and you'll be at **Point B**: The Lamplighter Pub's patio doors.

Gastown Twilight Saga Walk Point B
The Lamplighter Pub Patio
Where scenes of Riley leaving The Pike Pub in "Seattle" were shot.
http://donnellygroup.ca/locations/pubs/the-lamplighter/

Although the Lamplighter Pub's main entrance address is 92 Water Street, Vancouver, BC V6B, the Lamplighter Twilight Saga film site is on Abbott Street, at: **49.283718, -123.106414**—or (approximately) **212 Abbott St, Vancouver, BC V6B 1B2**

Very little information about Riley Biers' background, or his disappearance, is found in the *Eclipse* novel. Thanks to Stephenie Meyer's screenplay collaboration, however, we learn much more about Riley in the movie—which includes a fleeting glimpse of the flyer printed and distributed by his parents, describing where and when he went missing.

> "Riley Biers was last seen at 16:15 (4:15pm) on Friday, May 21 2010, walking towards the Pike Place Market."

[©2013 CD Miller—Seattle's Pike Pub]

Pike Place Market is a real-world place found in **Seattle, Washington** (*TTTS* Books One & Three, Site #1). The most popular Pike Place Market pub and brewery is **The Pike**.
http://www.pikebrewing.com/

[Eclipse screenshot (enhanced)]

The Lamplighter Pub's *Eclipse* film site is its Abbott Street patio doors. Alas, the neon bar signs and frosted glass with Celtic designs were set dressings removed after filming was finished. But, if you visit Seattle and snap a photo of The Pike's real-world neon sign, you can Photoshop it into your Lamplighter patio door pix.

[©2013 CD Miller]

Take turns with your companions going into the Lamplighter to obtain pix of each person exiting the pub via the patio doors (ala Riley in the screenshot). If you do this, it would be a nice gesture to purchase a sip of something while here.

Please Note: Beware of shooting photos with your reflection seen in the Lamplighter glass. Stand so that your reflection is obscured by one of the window frames, as CD Miller did when snapping the pic above.

Directions from Point B to Point C follow our **Trounce Alley** description, below.

Trounce Alley

Trounce Alley lies between Water and West Cordova streets, extending southeast from Cambie Street, *across* Abbott Street, and ending at Carrall Street. Blood Alley Square (**BAS**) is at the Carrall Street end of Trounce Alley.

Many Vancouver guidebooks and tourism companies refer to Trounce Alley as **Blood Alley**. They report that it once was a cobblestone street lined with butcher shops—its name originally deriving from all the blood that pooled in the street after butchers flushed out their shop floors each evening. These resources also claim that muggings and murders were commonplace in Blood Alley, contributing to the street's bloody history and resulting in rumors of "horror-filled psychic energy" that has allegedly generated multiple ghost sightings since the late 1800s. Additionally, Blood Alley Square is popularly described as having been the historic location of a public execution site—more blood.
http://www.vacationsmadeeasy.com/VancouverBC/pointsOfInterest/
GastownsHistoricBloodAlleyinVancouverBCCA.html
http://www.tourismvancouver.com/do/locals-insight/crowd-sourced/most-haunted-places/

Scholarly resources, however, soundly debunk all of these artistically-crafted rumors and reports. Chief among the scholars who have documented the history of Gastown is **John Atkin**, a civic historian and author who lives in Vancouver and is associated with the **Heritage Vancouver Society**. On his website, John clearly explains that Blood Alley and Blood Alley Square are fictional names assigned to spaces created during Gastown's heritage renovation and beautification project in the 1970s, in order to increase tourism.
http://www.johnatkin.com

http://www.johnatkin.com/blood.html
http://www.heritagevancouver.org/
http://www.vancouversun.com/news/news/4523360/story.html

In addition to realistically researching and writing about Vancouver's Gastown heritage sites, John Atkin conducts private tours of the area. Twilighters who have plenty of time to enjoy Gastown should consider booking one of John's historically accurate tours.

Another factually accurate Gastown tour is offered by the nearby **Vancouver Police Museum: Sins of the City, a Walking Tour on Vancouver's Shady Side. 240 East Cordova Street, Vancouver, BC V6A 1L3**
http://vancouverpolicemuseum.ca/sins-of-the-city-vice-dice-and-opium-pipes/

If you prefer the less factually-accurate drama and spooky thrills of a theatrical Gastown Ghost Tour, however, visit the links below.
http://forbiddenvancouver.ca/home/the-lost-souls-of-gastown/
https://www.facebook.com/pages/Forbidden-Vancouver-Walking-Tours/322483821123830
http://ghostlygastowntours.com/
https://www.facebook.com/GhostlyGastownTours

The Trounce Alley *Eclipse* Film Sites (Point C)
49.283424, -123.106567 — or 247 Abbott St, Vancouver, BC V6B 2K8

Thanks to movie magic, after exiting the Lamplighter (Seattle's Pike Place pub) — located at the northeastern corner of Abbott Street — Riley next is seen almost a block away, walking east through the western section of Trounce Alley that leads *toward* Abbott Street. Victoria begins her attack as he reaches Abbott Street.

🚶 Directions from Point B to Point C

After snapping pix at the Lamplighter patio doors, walk half-a-block south on the east side of Abbott Street to Trounce Alley. Once there, turn right and look across the street. The Trounce Alley entrance on the west side of Abbott Street is the first of our three Point C film sites. Snap your first Trounce Alley screenshot reproduction pix from the east side of Abbott Street.

[Eclipse screenshot (enhanced)]

Above is Victoria terrorizing Riley at vamp-speed, just after he reached Abbott Street from the western section of Trounce Alley. Below is what this site looked like in September of 2013.

[©2013 CD Miller]

The real-world alley entrance, the street lamps, and the **Bruce Eyewear** shop's window logos can be seen in the screenshot, as well as in the pix you'll snap here.

Next, cross Abbott Street to the Trounce Alley entrance on its west side (as seen above), walk a short distance *into* the alley, and about-face. Now you'll be seeing Riley's point of view immediately after leaving The Pike—just before Victoria began her bash-and-dash idea of good fun.

[Eclipse screenshot (enhanced) above; The real-world Trounce Alley view in 2013 (©CD Miller) below]

During Victoria's second bash-and-dash rush at Riley, she launched him all the way across Abbott Street and into the windows of the real-world **Montauk Sofa** store, seen at right, above.

[Eclipse Special Features screenshot segment (enhanced)]

Riley gamely got up and tried to run back to the west side of Abbott Street (presumably heading back to the Pike Pub), but Victoria bashed him again and he ended up running into the *eastern* section of Trounce Alley—toward Blood Alley Square.

[©2013 CD Miller]

And, that concludes the *Eclipse* Trounce Alley Point C film sites.

Why? Because, after running a few feet into the eastern section of Trounce Alley, Riley magically emerged many miles away in **Richmond** (a Vancouver suburb), on a dock at the **Gulf of Georgia Cannery** (Site #34).

🚶 Directions from Point C to Point D

Walk south on Abbott Street to West Pender Street. ♦ Turn right and walk a half block west to Beatty Street. ♦ Cross to the west side of Beatty Street, walk a half block southwest until you're at the alley just beyond a car park. ♦ About-face, and you'll be at Point D on the Gastown Twilight Saga Walk Map.

രജ്ഞ

Beatty Street (Point D)
538 Beatty Street, Vancouver, British Columbia V6B 1S5

In *Breaking Dawn* Part Two, Bella drove to Seattle to meet the mysterious J Jenks. Scenes of her parking outside their meeting place were filmed on **Beatty Street** in Vancouver. Interior scenes of Bella's J Jenks meeting, however, were shot in a restaurant of the **Roosevelt Hotel**—located in **New Orleans, Louisiana, USA** (*TTTS* Book Four).

[*Breaking Dawn* Part Two screenshot segment (enhanced) above. ©2013 CD Miller pic below]

After filming Bella parking her car, the camera paned up to reveal **Sun Tower**—a distinctive Vancouver heritage building.
http://suntowerbuilding.com/building/history/
http://en.wikipedia.org/wiki/Sun_Tower

From Sun Tower's website:

> "Sun Tower was built in 1912. The building was commissioned by L.D. Taylor, longtime mayor of Vancouver, to house The Vancouver World newspaper. W.T. Whiteway, the architect for the original Woodwards building, drafted the design. When it was completed, the 17-storey tower was the tallest building in all of the British Empire."

[*Breaking Dawn* Part Two screenshot segment (enhanced) above. ©2013 CD Miller pic below]

🚶 Directions from Point D to Point E

Resume walking southwest on Beatty Street for 2½ blocks to reach Robson Street. ♦ Turn right and walk northwest approximately 5 blocks to Seymour Street. ♦ Cross to the west side of Seymour, turn left and walk almost 1 block southwest. ♦ Just before reaching Smithe Street you'll see the **Orpheum Theatre**'s back entrance on your right—**Point E**.

[©2012 Xicotencatl]

About The Orpheum Theatre
http://vancouver.ca/parks-recreation-culture/the-orpheum.aspx
http://en.wikipedia.org/wiki/Orpheum_%28Vancouver%29
http://www.insidevancouver.ca/2014/07/12/new-all-access-tour-goes-inside-vancouvers-historic-orpheum-theatre/

An article written by Remy Scalza and published on the *Inside Vancouver* blog in July of 2014 (link above) described the Orpheum Theatre so well, we're simply going to quote it here.

> "When it opened its doors in 1927, the Orpheum was the biggest theatre in Canada, built with 3,000 seats at the astronomical cost of $1.25 million.
>
> Few expenses were spared by architect Marcus Priteca, who designed more than 220 theatres across North America. He built the Orpheum in a grand (albeit eclectic) style incorporating influences from Moroccan architecture, the Taj Mahal, Moorish arches and British heraldry, all layered on top of a Spanish Baroque style, with grand staircases, plenty of gold leaf and of course the Orpheum's giant gilded dome. …
>
> After vaudeville theatre died out in the 1930s, the Orpheum transitioned to a movie house. Promoters sometimes resorted to bizarre techniques to fill the cavernous venue, including parading a bull down Granville Street before the start of a Western [movie] and hiring actress Yvonne de Carlo (a Vancouver native who

would go on to star in The Munsters sitcom) to dance on stage before a Hawaiian movie. Occasionally, live acts performed too, including Frank Sinatra, who famously shattered his dressing room lights while practicing a golf swing.

Although the Orpheum limped along, in the 1970s its owners made the decision to gut it and turn it into a multiplex. Only a furious public protest saved one of the city's architectural treasures. ... In 1974, the City of Vancouver bought the theatre for $7.1 million. An extensive renovation ensued (involving the participation of some of the theatre's original designers from the 1920s, believe it or not) and the Orpheum was reopened in 1977 with a new entrance on Smithe Street.

Since then, it has been the permanent home of the Vancouver Symphony Orchestra and also hosted countless performances from some of the world's top music groups. Plus it served as [a film site for several episodes of] Battlestar Galactica."

Please Note: The 2004-2009 *Battlestar Galactica* TV series shared another Twilight Saga film site—one seen in *New Moon* and *Eclipse*. You'll find this information in the Coquitlam **Widgeon Slough Marsh** chapter (Site #26).

Visiting Orpheum Theatre Twilight Saga Film Sites is ... Somewhat Problematic

Scenes for *Breaking Dawn Part One* were filmed inside the Orpheum Theatre's performance area, as well as within a hallway and staircase found above the theatre's lobby. To get *into* the Orpheum Theatre and snap pix of these film sites, you must either attend an Orpheum Theatre performance or book a public tour.

Attend an Orpheum Theatre Performance

As the official home of the **Vancouver Symphony Orchestra**, and host to a plethora of other performing artists, every event offered at the Orpheum Theatre is a thoroughly enjoyable experience. We highly recommend attending a show in this fabulous theatre.

When attending an Orpheum Theatre show you can snap all the pix you want within hallways and staircases outside the performance area. The only photos you can take *within* the actual theatre space film site, however, are those snapped while the audience is filling the seats before the performance, or leaving after the final bows.

"**Performance Protocol:** Taking photographs and recording performances in theatres is not allowed unless authorized by the

promoter or producer. Cameras and recording devices may be
confiscated by theatre staff for the duration of the show."

The best thing about obtaining Twilight Saga screenshot reproduction pix
when attending an event is that there will be loads of people in the seats, and
your performance area pix will look almost exactly like the first two *Breaking
Dawn Part One* screenshots below.

Unfortunately, tickets to Orpheum Theatre events and performances
aren't cheap. The least expensive tickets generally range from $55 to $200,
with special act tickets sometimes costing between $184 and $464.

To learn what Orpheum Theatre events and performances are offered
during the dates of your Vancouver Twilight Saga trip, go to:
http://www.vancouver-theatre.com/theaters/orpheum-theater/theater.php

Book an Orpheum Theatre Public Tour

Public tours of the Orpheum Theatre are offered by the **BC Entertainment
Hall of Fame**, which happens to be housed *within* the Orpheum Theatre.
http://www.bcentertainmenthalloffame.com/

Here is part of their tour description:

"The 90-minute experience takes you right up to the catwalk near
the giant, iconic dome and down through subterranean hallways
where entertainment legends like Frank Sinatra, Jack Benny and
WC Fields once walked. All sorts of secrets are revealed about
the building on the tour which takes you through areas basically
unchanged since the late '20s."

In addition to the Orpheum Theatre public tours being extremely entertaining,
they are incredibly inexpensive: "a minimum **cash-only** donation" of $10
Canadian dollars per person. You'll pay for the tour ticket upon arrival.

Problematic Orpheum Theatre Tour Limitations

- To date, Orpheum Theatre public tours have only been offered in
  the months of **July and August**. This is because tours cannot be held
  during months when the theatre is terrifically busy. July and August
  are the "quietest" months of the year for the Orpheum.
- The tours are only offered once a day, on **Tuesdays**, **Thursdays**, and
  Saturdays.
- Although the tours are scheduled to start at 11am, **please arrive no
  later than 10:45am**. The theatre's doors are locked immediately after
  tour participants have been ushered inside. If you're late, you won't
  gain entrance.
- Children under the age of 12 are not allowed on the tours.

- Public Orpheum Theatre tours require a minimum of 12 pre-booked participants, and can accommodate a maximum of 30 people. Tickets are offered on a first-come, first-served basis, so be sure to reserve them ahead of time.
- The BC Entertainment Hall of Fame Orpheum Theatre Tour reservation line is only in operation during the months of July and August. Leave a message indicating the date you wish to join the tour—that is your reservation. You'll not receive a return call unless the tour is fully booked or cancelled on that day. **604-665-3470**

Please Note: Groups of 30 visitors *may* be able to book a private tour (for the same per-person donation) at other times of the year. Go to the BC Entertainment Hall of Fame website, click on the Contacts button, and send them an Email. The web master will relay your request to one of the board members and they will contact you.

About The Orpheum Theatre Twilight Saga Screenshots

Edward's *Breaking Dawn Part One* flashback involved an incident that took place during the years when he'd left Carlisle—1927 to 1931—and was feeding on humans whose thoughts indicated evil intent.
http://www.twilightlexicon.com/the-lexicon/timeline/

In his flashback, Edward was sitting in a movie theatre (the Orpheum Theatre's performance area), watching *Bride of Frankenstein*—the on-screen screams echoed by those of the audience.

Oddly enough, the 1920s were largely dominated by silent films and the *Bride of Frankenstein* wasn't released until 1935. Perhaps director Bill Condon felt that *Bride of Frankenstein* was a more visually and *acoustically* interesting "old" movie to use for these scenes. No matter why it was selected, we applaud his choice.

But, wait, there's more! The Orpheum Theatre didn't transition from a Vaudeville Theatre to a movie house until the mid-1930s. Thus, although *Bride of Frankenstein* is not an accurate fit with the Twilight Saga timeline, the movie's selection is entirely appropriate to the place where filming occurred.

Happily, none of this really matters.

What matters is that *BDp1* filming of Edward's flashback took place here in March of 2011. Twilighters who can get *into* the Orpheum Theatre can see and snap shots of the all the spaces where filming occurred.

The Orpheum Theatre Twilight Saga Screenshots

[Breaking Dawn Part One screenshot (enhanced)]

Distinctive architectural features observed on either side of the Orpheum Theatre's proscenium arch (the arch that frames the front of a stage) can be seen in the screenshot above. If snapped from the balcony, your shot of the stage will look exactly like the screenshot. If snapped from the main floor, it will look like the photo below.

[©2011 Michael Thoeny (segment) enhanced]

From wherever you snap it, consider Photoshopping a *Bride of Frankenstein* screenshot into the proscenium arch portion of your Orpheum Theatre's stage pic.

[Breaking Dawn Part One screenshot (enhanced)]

When snapping reproduction pix of the screenshot above in the Orpheum Theatre's balcony, use the emergency exit door to line up your shots. Unfortunately, the real-world emergency exit is crowned with a bright red Exit sign that you'll need to Photoshop out of your pix.

[©2013 Martin Knowles Photo/Media (segment) enhanced]

If you visit the Orpheum Theatre via a public tour instead of by attending a performance—when the seats are filled with people—you'll still be able to snap some fabulous photos. Every nook and cranny of this place is absolutely gorgeous!

[Breaking Dawn Part One screenshot (enhanced)]

After watching a woman leave the theatre during the movie, Edward follows. The screenshot above shows the woman walking through a balcony hallway that looks down on the Orpheum's lobby from the third level (the upper balcony).

[©2013 Martin Knowles Photo/Media (segment) enhanced]

The strange-looking, black apparatus seen in the third level balcony niche in the screenshot and real-world photo above is an old movie projector.

[Breaking Dawn Part One screenshot (enhanced)]

Next, the woman is seen walking through the third level hallway (balcony railing on the right), heading toward the Ladies' toilet. The crystal chandeliers seen in the screenshots above and below are particular to the upper level balcony.

[Breaking Dawn Part One screenshot (enhanced)]

Because the third level is open to the lobby on all four of its interior sides, you can snap the screenshot above from the hallway on the opposite side—which is where the cameras were positioned to shoot the scene above.

[©2007 Battlestar Galactica Season 3, Crossroads Part I screenshot segment (enhanced)]

Please Note: The Orpheum Theatre's third level hallway (balcony railing seen on the left, above) was also used to film footage for several episodes of the most recent *Battlestar Galactica* TV series (2004-2009). In fact, many more areas of the Orpheum Theatre can be seen in *Battlestar Galactica* (**BSG**) than in *BDp1*.
http://www.imdb.com/title/tt0407362/
http://en.battlestarwiki.org/wiki/Opera_House

If you're also a *Battlestar Galactica* fan, there are plenty of *BSG* screenshot reproductions to shoot when visiting. See the Supplement we created, containing a collection of *BSG* screenshots filmed in the Orpheum Theatre, freely posted on our website.
http://www.TourTheTwilightSaga.com/B2/BSGscreenshots.pdf

[Breaking Dawn Part One screenshots (enhanced), above and below.]

After the woman heads down some stairs to the Ladies' restroom, Edward's true prey is revealed. He wasn't following the woman. Edward was following a man who intended to attack the woman.

To see several Orpheum Theatre pix snapped by other Twilighters, go to:
http://twilightgirlportland.com/filming-location-bd-1-orpheum-theater/

> "Here are some photos that were taken inside of the theater. Thanks to my Twi friend for some of these as it was hard to get good photos with the lighting."

Visiting the Orpheum Theatre during Your Gastown Twilight Saga Walk

If you're lucky enough to be able to book an Orpheum Theatre performance or public tour when Twilighting in Vancouver, you probably won't be able to schedule your Orpheum Theatre visit during a Gastown Twilight Saga Walk. Not a problem. You can skip the Orpheum Theatre (Points E and F) by going directly from Point D to Point G.

Directions from Point D to Point G

🚶 Resume walking southwest on Beatty Street for one and one-half blocks to reach **West Georgia Street**. ♦ Turn right and walk northwest approximately eight blocks to Hornby Street. ♦ Turn left and walk a few steps southwest to **Point G**.

If you cannot gain entrance during your Vancouver visit, follow our directions below to achieve the best exterior Orpheum Theatre visit.

Directions from Point D to Point E

🚶 Resume walking southwest on Beatty Street for two and one-half blocks to reach Robson Street. ♦ Turn right and walk northwest approximately five blocks to Seymour Street. ♦ Cross to the west side of Seymour, turn left and walk almost one block southwest. ♦ Just before reaching Smithe Street you'll see the Orpheum Theatre's rear exit doors on your right—**Point E.**

[©2013 CD Miller]

The Orpheum Theatre Peek-Inside Place (Point E)
49.279868, -123.120235 (On Seymour Street, around the corner from 601 Smithe Street, Vancouver, BC V6B 1L7)

The glass doors of this exit allow you at least a glimpse of the interior grandeur seen on screen. To avoid glass glare problems, put the lens of your camera right up *against* the glass of this entrance.

🚶 Directions from Point E to Point F

Walk a few steps southwest to Smithe Street. ♦ Turn right and walk one block to Granville Street. ♦ Turn right and you'll be looking at **Point F.**

[©2013 Xicotencatl]

The Orpheum Theatre Marquee and Star Walk (Point F)
884 Granville Street, Vancouver, BC V6Z 1K3
http://en.wikipedia.org/wiki/Granville_Street
http://garrybrazzillphotography.com/granville-street-vancouver-history/

The iconic Orpheum Theatre marquee is one of only a few vintage neon marquees that have survived on the section of Granville Street still known as **Theatre Row**. Although photos of the Orpheum Theatre marquee aren't related to Twilight Saga screenshots, they're still a marvelous souvenir of your Vancouver, BC, Twilight trek.

[Wikipedia Source http://www.firstnations.de/] [©2010 Joe Mabel]

Below the Orpheum's marquee you'll find the BC Entertainment Hall of Fame's **Star Walk**. Three blocks long, the Star Walk includes more than 200 plaques honoring British Columbians who have made an outstanding contribution to the Canadian entertainment industry. You may be surprised at the number of names you recognize.

http://www.miss604.com/2007/12/granville-street-starwalk-and-redesign.html
http://www.bcentertainmenthalloffame.com/agency.php?view=roster

🚶 Directions from Point F to Point G

Walk one block northeast on Granville Street to Robson Street. ◆ Turn left and walk two blocks northwest to Hornby Street. ◆ Turn right and walk northeast for almost a block, watching across the street (on your left) for the **Hotel Vancouver** valet parking entrance, as seen below.

[©2013 CD Miller]

As soon as you see it, look right to find the **Edward VII Memorial** (below), and you've reached **Point G**.

[©2013 Google Street View segment (enhanced)]

Hornby Street Film Site (Point G)
49.283596,-123.12035 — or 700 Hornby St, Vancouver, BC V6E

Rosalie Lillian Hale was born in Rochester, New York, in 1915. In 1933 she became engaged to Royce King. Considered a "great catch" by local socialites, Royce actually was a repulsively spoiled Rochester rich boy. While walking home one night, Rosalie accidentally encountered Royce and his friends enjoying a drunken debauch. Following Royce's lead, they abused and severely beat her, then left her for dead. Alerted by the scent of fresh blood, Carlisle discovered Rosalie's unconscious and dying body. Although he couldn't ask her permission, Carlisle took pity on her and changed Rosalie into a vampire.
http://www.twilightlexicon.com/the-lexicon/timeline/

Rosalie's Rochester Attack flashback scenes were filmed on a corner of what originally was Vancouver's Provincial Courthouse, built between 1905 and 1913. Since 1983, this heritage building has been home to the **Vancouver Art Gallery**. If you have plenty of time and an interest in art, the Vancouver Art Gallery is a marvelous non-Twilight tourist destination.
http://www.vanartgallery.bc.ca
http://en.wikipedia.org/wiki/Vancouver_Art_Gallery

According to *Twilight Saga Eclipse: The Official Illustrated Movie Companion* by Mark Cotta Vaz:

> "When [Eclipse] principal photography began, the production had not yet locked into an exterior location for [Rosalie's Rochester attack flashback scenes] … Vancouver wasn't the best city for 1930s period architecture, although there were 'very small pockets,' Paul Austerberry noted. … 'We scoured the city, and it turned out the right location was right under our noses.'
>
> Downtown, right by the Hotel Vancouver, was the Vancouver Art Gallery, housed in a turn-of-the-century building. … 'The front of the Art Gallery had modern sculptures and fountains,' said Austerberry, 'but we used the side of the building … diagonally opposite the Hotel Vancouver, which was mostly intact, periodwise.' …
>
> The production design team and the art department also added period lighting fixtures that Javier Aguirresarobe could use as practical foreground lighting elements."

[Eclipse Special Features screenshot (enhanced)]

Hotel Vancouver's valet entrance and the Edward VII memorial are clearly recognized in an *Eclipse* DVD Special Features section that includes filming footage. Although your reproductions of the screenshot above won't include vintage automobiles, they also won't be marred by movie equipment.

[Eclipse screenshot (enhanced)]

Set up your reproductions of the screenshot above at the Vancouver Art Gallery corner just behind the memorial. The window is still there, but the lamp post was a set piece.

🚶 Directions from Point G to Point H

Walk a few steps northeast on Hornby Street to the West Georgia Street intersection. ♦ Turn left and walk half-a-block northwest to the front entrance of the **Fairmont Hotel Vancouver**.

[©2013 Google Street View segment (enhanced)]

The Fairmont Hotel Vancouver (Point H)
900 West Georgia Street, Vancouver, British Columbia, Canada V6C 2W6
http://www.fairmont.com/hotel-vancouver/

Fair Warning! You'll probably not be able to gain access to this film site. But, we found its story so interesting, we decided to hope for the best.

From the *Eclipse* script:

> ROSALIE: I did get revenge on them... one at a time.
> (ever-so-slight smile)
> I saved Royce for last... so he'd know I was coming. ...
> I was a little... theatrical back then.

[Eclipse Special Features screenshot segment (enhanced)]

Scenes of Rosalie exacting her "theatrical" final revenge on Royce were shot on the 14th floor of the Fairmont Hotel Vancouver—specifically, in the **Sitting Room** of the **Lieutenant Governor's Suite**, room number 1404.

We learned early on that Hotel Vancouver's 14th floor was an interior *Eclipse* film site based on several Internet sources, the chief of which was an article published in July of 2010: *Eclipse Production Notes: Making Eclipse*.
http://serdar-hizli-art.com/twilightsaga/2010/07/eclipse-production-notes-making-eclipse/

> "The challenge for us was trying to find a period-looking hotel that hadn't been renovated. The 14th floor in the Hotel Vancouver is pretty much intact from the 1930s. We just had to do some slight changes to accommodate our scene and bring in Art Deco [hotel bedroom] furnishings."

We didn't obtain confirmation of the Lieutenant Governor's Suite Sitting Room being the film site, however, until CD Miller stumbled upon the **50 Shades Girl Portland** fan blogsite in December of 2014.
http://50shadesgirlportland.com/?cat=14
http://www.imdb.com/title/tt2322441/
http://en.wikipedia.org/wiki/Fifty_Shades_of_Grey

50 Shades Girl Portland gained access to the Hotel Vancouver's Lieutenant Governor's Suite (LGS) in October of 2014. The photos she snapped and posted online were what confirmed the LGS Sitting Room as being the film site for Rosalie's Final Revenge on Royce.

BTW: We highly recommend visiting the **Twilight Girl Portland** fan blogsite—run by the same person. CD Miller didn't find this site until *after* discovering her 50 Shades Girl Portland blogsite.
http://twilightgirlportland.com/

Please Be Warned! You'll spend hours and hours enjoying the pix that Twilight Girl Portland (**TGP**) has snapped at the tons of Twilight Saga film sites she's visited, and reading all the info she offers for each site.

[©2014 *50 Shades Girl Portland* photo segment (enhanced)]

Above is TGP's pic of the interior side of the two sets of double doors that lead into the LGS Sitting Room. Note that this side of the doors contain strips of blonde inlaid-wood. Also note the unique pattern of the sitting room's wall-to-wall carpet.

[Eclipse Special Features screenshot segment (enhanced)]

In the *Eclipse* Special Features screenshot above you can see that production designers applied extra blonde inlaid-wood embellishments to the inside of the doors on the filming side of the sitting room. Next, look at the carpet. The wall-to-wall carpet found in the real-world sitting room is visible on the right. At left, you can see that a section of different carpet was laid down on the filming side.

Additionally, a '30s era wardrobe cabinet was positioned between the sitting room's two sets of double doors to provide a break that would *suggest a wall* for the filming side, thus diminishing the size of the hotel room seen on screen.

One of the biggest benefits of filming in *half* of Hotel Vancouver's LGS sitting room is having plenty of space to position bulky cameras and lighting equipment. Had a small hotel room been used for the film site, camera angles would have been severely limited.

[©Fairmont Hotel Vancouver]

Opposite the two sets of double doors leading into the real-world LGS sitting room is a wall containing two large windows. Positioned on either side of a wood-mantled fireplace, each window is set within a deep, wood-paneled alcove.

[Eclipse Special Features screenshot segment (enhanced)]

One of these windows—with its distinctive alcove—can be seen in the *Eclipse* Special Features screenshot above.

Although the furniture added for Royce's hotel room is long gone, if you can gain access to the LGS sitting room on Hotel Vancouver's 14th floor, you'll enjoy snapping photos where filming took place.

If you only can gain access to the 14th floor, the screenshot below is all you'll be able to shoot.

[Eclipse screenshot (enhanced)]

Brief scenes of three Rochester police officers guarding the door to Royce's hotel room—guards easily (and noisily) taken out by Rosalie prior to her theatrical entrance—were shot in the hallway of the 14th floor.

Besides installing blonde inlaid-wood embellishments on the doors' exterior side (just like what was added to the door's interior side), filmmakers mounted period wall sconces on either side of the doors, along with a couple chairs and potted plants.

[©2014 **50 Shades Girl Portland** photo segment (enhanced)]

Happily, as you can see in TGP's real-world 14th floor hallway pic of the LGS sitting room doors, the iconic Hotel Vancouver room number plaques are exactly the same as those seen on screen.

Visiting the Lieutenant Governor's Suite Sitting Room

Alas, the only sure way to gain access is to book the sitting room—something likely to cost around $600 a night during the off-season, possibly up to $1000 a night in the summer. BTW, that tariff does not include booking the attached suite.

As for simply visiting the 14th floor, **a room key card is required to use Hotel Vancouver elevators.** Thus, you'll have to book a room *somewhere* in the hotel. The cheapest rooms range from around $260 per night during the off-season, approximately $500 per night in the summer.

Because she's a prominent blogger, 50 Shades Girl Portland (aka, Twilight Girl Portland) arranged her sitting room tour by calling ahead of time and speaking to the Public Relations staff. If you are a similarly prominent blogger, call them and ask to set up a tour.

Happily, any intrepid Twilighter can always toss the dice and chat up the Hotel Vancouver Concierge. *If* the sitting room is unbooked, and *if* the Concierge has some free time, you *may* be able to get her/him to take you there. After all, it doesn't hurt to ask for a tour.

ᘓᘔᘓ

What about the Other Rosalie Flashback Film Site?

According to the 2010 *Eclipse Production Notes: Making Eclipse* article, the sunny park portions of Rosalie's Rochester flashback were filmed within the vast expanse of **VanDusen Botanical Gardens**.
5251 Oak Street, Vancouver, BC V6M 4H1, Canada
http://vandusengarden.org/
http://en.wikipedia.org/wiki/VanDusen_Botanical_Garden

Sadly, nothing seen in those scenes can still be found in these gorgeous gardens. Thus, even though they aren't found within Gastown or Downtown Vancouver, the VanDusen Botanical Gardens *Eclipse* film site is only mentioned in this chapter.

[Eclipse Special Features screenshot segment (enhanced)]

We contacted Corinne Johnston, the VanDusen Garden Facilities Rental Coordinator, in 2014. She and her staff immediately recognized the deleted Rosalie-Admires-Baby scenes' background. Unfortunately, none of them recognized the fence and lamp posts seen in the Rosalie-Strolling-With-Royce scenes. Thus, they must have been set pieces.

The "scanty record" created by Corinne's predecessor indicates that *some sort* of movie filming took place on "August 24-28, 2009," in a northwestern area of the **Great Lawn**. This timeframe is consistent with *Eclipse* filming, but no one currently working for VanDusen Gardens knows precisely where the film site is or what was filmed here.

[Eclipse Special Features screenshot segment (enhanced)]

According to Corinne and her helpful staff, the screenshot above was shot somewhere along the northeastern curve of Heron Lake, "near the Giant Redwoods."

Garden-loving Twilighters who will be driving to the film sites at **Burrard Bridge** (Site #33) and **Gulf of Georgia Cannery** (Site #34) can visit VanDusen Botanical Gardens *between* those stops. Twihards who visit will find the northeastern curve of Heron Lake—which is *huge*—on the VanDusen Botanical Gardens map, available online or on site.
http://vandusengarden.org/visit/plan-your-visit/vbg-map

[Google Maps segments married & enhanced, ©2013 Google]
http://www.TourTheTwilightSaga.com/B2/VBCtsMaps.pdf

When finished at the **Fairmont Hotel Vancouver** (Point H), **your Gastown Twilight Saga Walk is done**—apart from returning to the car park, or walking to a station where you can reach your next destination via public transportation.

🚆 Directions from Point H to CCS

If traveling on the **Canada Line**, the closest station is **Vancouver City Centre Station**, a 4 minute walk.

🚶 Walk 2½ blocks southeast on West Georgia Street. ♦ When you reach Granville Street, look to your right and you'll see the City Centre Station entrance.

🚆 Directions from Point H to GS

If traveling the **Expo** or **Millennium Lines**, head to **Granville Station**, a 5 minute walk.

🚶 Walk 2½ blocks southeast on West Georgia Street to Granville Street. ♦ Turn left and you'll see the Granville Station entrance across the street, on your right.

🚆 Directions from Point H to WS

If you prefer to enjoy a 10 minute Downtown Vancouver stroll back to the **Waterfront Station**—where you can catch **Expo**, **Millennium**, *or* **Canada Line** trains—below is the most direct route:

🚶 Walk 2½ blocks southeast on West Georgia Street to Granville Street. ♦ Turn left and walk 4 blocks northeast to West Cordova Street. You'll see the Waterfront Station across the street, on your right.

🚗 Directions from Point H to Point I

As you can see on our Gastown Twilight Saga Walk map, there are numerous possible routes for returning to the **Gastown Easy Park** facility (Point I) from Hotel Vancouver—all of which take about 18 minutes to walk if you don't stop anywhere. The route we identify simply guides you down some streets you've not yet explored and may enjoy.

🚶 Walk 2½ blocks southeast on West Georgia Street to Granville Street. ♦ Turn left and walk 1 block northeast to Dunsmuir Street. ♦ Turn right and walk 4 blocks southeast to Hamilton Street. ♦ Turn left and walk a couple blocks northeast to West Hastings Street. ♦ Turn right to walk a few steps southeast to Cambie Street. ♦ Turn left and walk a block northeast to Cordova Street. ♦ Turn right and you'll see the West Cordova Street Easy Park car and pedestrian entrance on your left.

32

Stanley Park

A Skip-It Film Site, *BUT!*

http://www.infovancouver.com/things-to-see-and-do/downtown-vancouver/stanley-park
http://vancouver.ca/parks-recreation-culture/stanley-park.aspx
http://www.tourismvancouver.com/do/explore/stanley-park-complete-guide/
http://en.wikipedia.org/wiki/Stanley_Park

Google Maps & SatNav/GPS: 735 Stanley Park Drive, Vancouver, BC V6G 3E2

Stanley Park Hours of Operation: Being city-owned, Stanley Park is open 24/7, and admission to all public areas is free.

Visit Time: SKIP this site if you're only interested in recognizable Twilight Saga film sites. If you're eager to enjoy one of Vancouver's most world-famous attractions—something we highly recommend—schedule 2 hours in Stanley Park, 3-4 hours if you'll also be visiting the Vancouver Aquarium.

[©2011 YVR Shoots photo (enhanced)]

On April 18th, 2011, the *Breaking Dawn* Part Two second unit set up in Stanley Park to film Kristen Stewart as newly-made vampire Bella doing vamp-fast running stunts with a forest background. In actuality, she was running on a treadmill towed down a lane by a camera truck. The filming location was an interior Stanley Park road that stretches between the Vancouver Aquarium and the Brockton Oval—a Rugby Field.
http://vancouverisawesome.com/2011/04/28/yvrshoots-breaking-dawns-vampire-running-in-stanley-park/
http://www.brocktonpavilion.ca/

[©2013 CD Miller]

Because the photo above represents all you'll see at this film site, Stanley Park earns a **Skip It** rating as a Twilight Saga film site.

However! Stanley Park is one of Vancouver's most world-famous attractions. Twilighters with time to explore Stanley Park will thoroughly enjoy it—especially the **First Nations Art and Totem Poles** display and the **Vancouver Aquarium**.

To help you find the BDp2 film site and other places in Stanley Park, we modified a section of the Vancouver Board of Parks and Recreation's 2014 Official Map & Guide.
http://vancouver.ca/files/cov/Stanely-park-map-2014.pdf
http://vancouver.ca/parks-recreation-culture/printable-map-of-stanley-park.aspx

You will find the **Stanley Park Film Site & First Nations Totems** map we created in the **Vancouver, BC Twilight Saga Maps PDF** freely posted on our website.

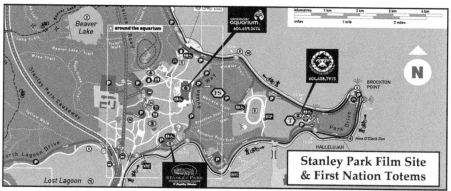

[©2014 Vancouver Board of Parks & Recreation map segment (modified & enhanced)]
http://www.TourTheTwilightSaga.com/B2/VBCtsMaps.pdf

The Stanley Park Film Site & First Nation Totems Map Key

FS: *Breaking Dawn* Part Two film site

T: First Nations Totem Poles & Art Display

Black-Circled P Symbols: Pay Parking

Red-Circled S Symbols: Vancouver Trolley Stanley Park Shuttle Stops

1: Stanley Park Information Booth and Horse-Drawn Carriage Kiosk

2: Legends of the Moon Gift Shop

3: Malkin Bowl / Theatre Under the Stars
http://malkinbowl.com/

4: Stanley Park Miniature Train Station
http://vancouver.ca/parks-recreation-culture/stanley-park-miniature-train.aspx

5. [Not within the pictured area]

6: Vancouver Aquarium

For all other symbols and numbers, please see the Vancouver Board of Parks and Recreation's Official Map & Guide.

[©2010 Joan Felip] [©2006 Peter Graham]

The Stanley Park First Nations Art and Totem Display

http://vancouver.ca/parks-recreation-culture/totems-and-first-nations-art.aspx
http://vancouver.about.com/od/historylandmarks/p/stanleytotems.htm
http://www.tourismvancouver.com/do/explore/stanley-park-complete-guide/sightseeing-spots/

Carving magnificent totems (stylized images) of spirit animals is an essential aspect of the historic culture of Jacob's people, as described in the Site #22 Quileute Reservation chapter of *Tour the Twilight Saga* Book One—the Olympic Peninsula. In 2009, the Quileute Tribal Council created a **Tribal School Cultural Center for Carvers** and hired a Master Carver to teach the art of Northwest Native American wood carving to all students and tribal members interested in learning the skills.

Stanley Park's fabulous First Nations Totem Poles offer Twilighters an opportunity to view Northwestern Native American animal totems similar to those carved by the Quileutes. Please keep in mind, however, that the Quileute people did not create "totem poles" until recent years, when tourists began clamoring for them.

[©2014 Ruth McCann]

Legends of the Moon Gift Shop
http://www.legendsofthemoon.com/

Merely a few feet from the totem poles, the gift shop is open daily from 9am to 4pm.

> "At Legends of the Moon, you'll find locally produced giftware, jewelry, hand-crafted products, clothing, accessories and novelty souvenirs. ... we offer a wonderful assortment of high-quality First Nations and Canadian-themed gifts and souvenirs."

Visiting the First Nations Totem Poles and Legends of the Moon gift shop is free, as is wandering anywhere else in Stanley Park's public areas. Some Twilighters, however, may be interested in touring Stanley Park via a Horse-Drawn Carriage!

[©2014 Mike Harding]

Stanley Park Horse-Drawn Tours
http://www.stanleyparktours.com/

> "Step aboard one of our old-fashioned horse-drawn vehicles and meander in comfort through the natural beauty of Stanley Park, Vancouver's thousand acre wonderland. A professional guide fully narrates the tour which highlights Deadman's Island, Vancouver's Harbour, Lions Gate Bridge, a Coastal Red Cedar Forest, and includes stops at the Totem Poles, the Girl in a Wet Suit Statue, the S.S. Empress of Japan Figurehead, and the Rose Garden."

Stanley Park Horse-Drawn Tours operate from March to October and last at least an hour. The 2015 fares are listed below.

- Adults: $34.99
- Seniors (65+) and Students: $33.29
  ID may be required to obtain a Senior or Student discount.
- Children aged 4-12: $16.99
- Tots 3 & Under: FREE, when not occupying a seat if otherwise needed.

[©2005 Stan Shebs (enhanced)]

The Vancouver Aquarium
http://www.vanaqua.org/
http://en.wikipedia.org/wiki/Vancouver_Aquarium
http://www.tourismvancouver.com/do/activities-attractions/attractions/vancouver-aquarium-guide/

"The Vancouver Aquarium is a recognized leader in connecting people to our natural world. As a self-supporting, non-profit association, the Aquarium is dedicated to effecting the conservation of aquatic life through display and interpretation, education, research and direct action. More than 35 million people have visited the Aquarium since our opening in 1956. Located in Stanley Park, we're open to visitors from around the world 365 days a year. ...
       The Vancouver Aquarium is suited to all ages and interests. ... Tickets can be purchased in person and online."

Discussing all the marvelous exhibits, galleries, and shows offered at the Vancouver Aquarium would fill an entire chapter. If you love aquariums, the decision is simple: go to the aquarium's website and buy your ticket!

If you're not sure whether you want to visit the aquarium while in Vancouver, get comfy and visit their website. You can spend an hour or more simply exploring all the Vancouver Aquarium attractions available *online*.

Judith S visited in August of 2014 and penned the TripAdvisor review below.

> "This is not an inexpensive place to visit but a good value for your dollar and the educational opportunities for children are very good. There is something for all ages and the 4D show is excellent with great special effects. The expansion to the aquarium has been very well done with a true west coast flare and a very nice place to relax with some refreshment inside or out. Not only is it interesting as an aquarium but a great place for close up photography especially in the fish department - the colors are exquisite. The shows are outside but even for a rainy day activity this is an excellent place to visit."

To read more TripAdvisor Vancouver Aquarium reviews, go to:
http://www.tripadvisor.com/Attraction_Review-g154943-d155848-Reviews-Vancouver_
Aquarium-Vancouver_British_Columbia.html

The outside shows Judith refers to are the multiple live demonstrations offered throughout the day—all of which are included in the Vancouver Aquarium admission price. The schedule changes daily and seasonally, based on the needs of the animals. Frequently offered demonstrations feature Beluga whales, dolphins, sea lions, sharks, penguins, sea otters, and more.
http://www.vanaqua.org/experience/shows

What are the 4D Shows?

They are films shown in an IMAX film with 3-D visual effects and much, much more!

> "Visiting an IMAX theatre is one thing, but the Vancouver Aquarium's 4D Experience takes it a step further—the fourth dimension being the addition of sensory effects such as mist, scents, lighting and wind. These are coupled with a state-of-the-art theatre system that displays some of the best nature documentaries and films in the world, including the Planet Earth series."

> http://www.vanaqua.org/experience/shows/4-d-theatre-shows

Vancouver Aquarium 4D shows also are included in the admission price.

Vancouver Aquarium 2015 Winter/Spring Admission Prices:

- Adult: $29
- Senior (65+): $20
- Student (18+ with a valid student card from any post-secondary education institution): $20
- Youth (13-18): $20
- Accompanied Child 4 to 12 y/o: $15
- Accompanied Child 3 y/o & Under: FREE
  http://www.vanaqua.org/visit/tickets

If you decide to visit Stanley Park's Vancouver Aquarium, be sure to schedule at least 2 hours in the aquarium—3 or 4 hours if you'll have children with you.

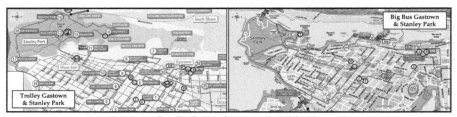

http://www.TourTheTwilightSaga.com/B2/VBCtsMaps.pdf

Going to Stanley Park

 Use the Vancouver Hop-On/Hop-Off Busses or Trolley

Whether driving or using public transportation to reach downtown Vancouver, you may enjoy riding the Vancouver Hop-On/Hop-Off busses or Trolley to visit Stanley Park. Convenient and scenic, these guided tours can be fun. Our **Vancouver, BC Twilight Saga Maps PDF** includes maps made from sections of the Hop-On/Hop-Off bus and Trolley routes, with our Gastown and Downtown Vancouver (Site #31) Twilight Saga Site identifiers added—as well as the identifiers for Twilicious places-of-interest found in Stanley Park.

https://westcoastsightseeing.com/hop-on-hop-off/
http://www.vancouvertrolley.com/tours/hop-on-hop-off

Within Stanley Park You Can Ride the Vancouver Trolley Stanley Park Shuttle

To learn more about the **Stanley Park Shuttle** visit its website:
http://vancouvertrolley.com/tour/stanley-park-shuttle

"The Stanley Park Shuttle offers the most flexible transportation to 15 of the most popular stops in Stanley Park. Sit back, relax, take in the sights, sounds, iconic views and countless photo opportunities on our old-fashioned San Francisco-style trolleys. The 45-minute tour is narrated and you can get on or off at any stop. There are well-marked Stanley Park Shuttle signs along the route."

🚗 Driving to Stanley Park

The park's main entrance is at the west end of Georgia Street.

If approaching from the east (from downtown Vancouver), head west on Georgia Street—aka the BC-99 highway—watching on your right for "Stanley Park Vancouver Aquarium" signs. Take the Stanley Park exit and continue northwest until you turn right to enter the park.

If approaching from North Vancouver, things are a little more complicated. Head for Lions Gate Bridge to cross Vancouver Harbor and reach Stanley Park Causeway. Stay in the right lane as you continue south on Stanley Park Causeway—*passing* the main park entrance (which you'll see on your left) until Stanley Park Causeway becomes West Georgia Street. Watch for Denman Street on your right and turn right there. Take the next left onto Alberni Street. Pass Bidwell Street and take the next left onto Cardero Street. Go to West Georgia Street and turn left into the far right lane. Watch for the "Stanley Park Exit Only" lane on your right. Take that exit and continue northwest until you turn right to enter the park.

[©2000 Besharat Friars Architects]

Google Maps & SatNav/GPS
Stanley Park Information Booth and Horse-Drawn Carriage Kiosk:
735 Stanley Park Drive, Vancouver, BC V6G 3E2

Enter Stanley Park by turning right from the exit lane off of West Georgia Street. At the first roundabout, take the first right onto Stanley Park Drive. Soon after driving under an overpass you'll see the information booth ahead, on your left. Turn left into the car park *before* the information booth. The Horse-Drawn Carriage kiosk is just beyond the information booth.

The Vancouver Aquarium
845 Avison Way, Vancouver, BC V6G 3E2

After passing the Information booth on Stanley Park Drive, take the next left onto Avison Way. Drive north on Avison Way until you see the Vancouver Aquarium on your left. Turn right for parking.

First Nations Totems and Legends of the Moon Parking Lot
49.298057, -123.122446 (The gift shop's address doesn't quite get you there.)

After passing the Information booth, continue driving east on Stanley Park Drive until you see a large car park on your left.

Stanley Park Car Parks
Hourly and Daily parking passes are available.
http://vancouver.ca/parks-recreation-culture/stanley-park-parking.aspx

"If you are planning to drive to Stanley Park for the day, consider buying a daily parking pass. A daily parking pass lets you move your car and park at any location within Stanley Park. Hourly parking passes are valid only in the lots or spaces closest to the parking meter where you purchased the ticket. ... Parking Regulations are strictly enforced."

Burrard Bridge
A Skip-It *Eclipse* Film Site
http://en.wikipedia.org/wiki/Burrard_Bridge

Google Maps & SatNav/GPS: 1604-1606 Seaside Bicycle Route, Vancouver, BC V6J 1A9 (The closest car park entrance address.)

Hours of Operation: Because it is adjacent to a city-owned recreation area, this film site is open 24/7 — visiting after dark, however, is discouraged.

Visit Time: 30 minutes is more than enough time to walk to the film site from the closest car park, snap a few pix, and walk back to your car.

⊂ℨ℞∽

At the end of Jasper's flashback scenes in *Eclipse*, the movie segued into a bizarre and scary Bella dream sequence. She awoke with the realization that Victoria was behind the Seattle killings and the creation of a Newborn Army.

[Eclipse screenshot (enhanced)]

The next scene was of Riley delivering the latest victim to Victoria so that she could turn him. The setting was under some kind of bridge. Later, scenes at the same location were preceded by a shot of the **Seattle Center Monorail** passing overhead.

[Eclipse screenshot (enhanced)]

As reported by Lainey Gossip on August 21st, 2009:

> "Last night the Twilight Eclipse crew was back to work shooting a 'Seattle' scene under a [Vancouver, BC] bridge with Bryce Dallas Howard and Xavier Samuel as 'Victoria and Riley.' Victoria seduces Riley so that he'll carry out her orders to make new vampires. As you can see, they've wigged out Bryce's hair to resemble Rachelle Lefevre's."
>
> http://www.laineygossip.com/Bryce-Dallas-Howard-as-Victoria-shoots-seduction-scene-with-Xavier-Samuel-as-Riley-on-Vancouver-set/14333

This film site is located next to **Vanier Park**, beneath the south shore end of the **Burrard Street Bridge** that crosses **False Creek**—a small inlet between the west end of downtown Vancouver and southern parts of the city.
http://www.greatervancouverparks.com/Vanier01.html
http://en.wikipedia.org/wiki/False_Creek

☹ The Burrard Bridge Film Site Earns a Skip-It Rating Because:

- The film site has been cleaned up and no longer looks *anything* like what was seen on screen.

That said, there are other attractions in this area that may be of interest to Vancouver-visiting Twilighters, and the Burrard Bridge film site is only a short walk from any of them.

[Google Street View image segment (enhanced), ©2014 Google]

The H.R. MacMillan Space Centre and The Museum of Vancouver

http://www.spacecentre.ca/
http://en.wikipedia.org/wiki/H._R._MacMillan_Space_Centre
http://www.museumofvancouver.ca/
http://en.wikipedia.org/wiki/Museum_of_Vancouver

Google Maps & SatNav/GPS: 1100 Chestnut Street, Vancouver, BC, V6J 3J9

These two amazing Vanier Park attractions are housed in opposite wings of a huge building that has a large 24-hour pay-and-display car park.

Vancouver Maritime Museum

http://www.vancouvermaritimemuseum.com/
http://en.wikipedia.org/wiki/Vancouver_Maritime_Museum

Google Maps & SatNav/GPS: 1905 Ogden Ave, Vancouver, BC V6J 1A3, Canada

Vanier Park is also home to the Vancouver Maritime Museum, which is not far from the MacMillan Space Centre and the Museum of Vancouver.

Twilighters interested in visiting all of these museums can save money by purchasing a **Vanier Park ExplorePass**. Valid for one entry to each of the three Vanier Park museum attractions, the ExplorePass can be purchased at any of them, and you don't have to visit all of them in one day. You can take three or more days to use your admission tickets.
http://www.museumofvancouver.ca/about/explorepass

[©2015 Bard on the Beach]

The Bard on the Beach Shakespeare Festival
http://www.bardonthebeach.org/

Twilighters who also happen to be Shakespeare fans will thoroughly enjoy attending a performance or special event at the Bard on the Beach festival offered each summer.

> "**Bard on the Beach** is one of Canada's largest not-for-profit, professional Shakespeare Festivals. Presented in a magnificent setting on the waterfront in Vancouver's Vanier Park, the Festival offers Shakespeare plays, related dramas, and several special events in two performance tents from June through September."

Finding the Film Site

To help Vanier Park attraction-visiting Twilighters—as well as Twihards divinely inspired to visit a Skip It site—to find the Burrard Bridge film site, we created a **Burrard Bridge Film Site Area** map. It is included in the **Vancouver, BC Twilight Saga Maps PDF** freely posted on our website.

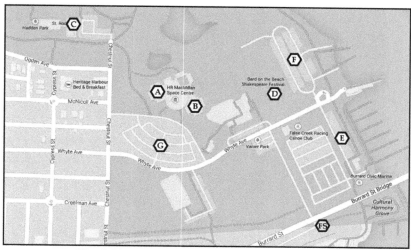

[Google Maps segments (married & enhanced), ©2015 Google]
http://www.TourTheTwilightSaga.com/B2/VBCtsMaps.pdf

The Twilight Saga Burrard Bridge Film Site Area Map Key

FS: The Burrard Bridge *Eclipse* film sites

A: H.R. MacMillan Space Centre

B: Museum of Vancouver

C: Vancouver Maritime Museum

D: Bard on the Beach Shakespeare Festival

E: Burrard Civic Marina car park

F: Vanier Park car park

G: MacMillan Space Centre & Museum of Vancouver car park

Google Maps & SatNav/GPS: 1604-1606 Seaside Bicycle Route, Vancouver, BC V6J 1A9

The address above will lead you to the entrance of car parks E and F. Turn right for the car park closest to the film site (E). Turn left for the car park closest to Bard on the Beach (F).

The directions below are written to guide Twilighters who park in the **Burrard Civic Marina** car park to the film site. If you park elsewhere, simply use our Burrard Bridge Film Site Area map to walk to that car park (E) and then follow our directions.

http://vancouver.ca/streets-transportation/burrard-civic-marina.aspx

[©2013 CD Miller]

Immediately after turning right at the Burrard Civic Marina car park entrance, stop and purchase a ticket. Park close to the Burrard Street Bridge.

The Burrard Bridge Civic Marina building is at the south end of the parking lot. It has public toilets, a water fountain, a pay phone, and drinks vending machines.

Follow the pedestrian/bike path that leads south from the parking lot.

[©2013 CD Miller]

After passing beneath Burrard Bridge, turn right and walk southwest on the pedestrian path. When you reach the very last section of the bridge's support columns you'll be at the platform where "Riley delivering the latest victim to Victoria" scenes were shot.

[©2013 CD Miller]

As it happens, city workers were in the process of cleaning-up this site when CD Miller visited in September of 2013, and she wasn't allowed under the bridge to take photos.

When you visit, however, there should be no impediment to snapping platform pix from beneath the bridge. And, perhaps new graffiti will adorn the walls behind the platform, so that your photos look more like the screen-shot seen at the beginning of this chapter.

To find the film site for "Victoria seduces Riley so that he'll carry out her orders to make new vampires" scenes (the second screenshot seen at the beginning of this chapter), simply head back the way you came, until you reach the next section of bridge support columns.

[Eclipse Special Features screenshot segment (enhanced)]

121

Because other Burrard Bridge support column sections cannot be seen from the area beneath the southernmost support columns, these scenes had to have been filmed in the underpass just north of that section's platform. If you have Riley and Victoria stand-ins, the shots you take here will be the best possible screenshot reproduction pix available.

If you are able to snap photos that look like any of the screenshots above, please share your Burrard Bridge film site photos with us on Facebook. https://www.facebook.com/pages/Tour-The-Twilight-Saga/533851833326773

Or, email them directly to CD Miller: **chas@novelholiday.com**

34

Steveston Village, Richmond, British Columbia

Gulf of Georgia Cannery *Eclipse* Film Sites

http://www.steveston.bc.ca/
http://en.wikipedia.org/wiki/Steveston,_British_Columbia
http://www.richmond.ca/home.htm
http://en.wikipedia.org/wiki/Richmond,_British_Columbia

Google Maps & SatNav/GPS: 12138 Fourth Ave, Richmond, British Columbia V7E—do not add 3T4 to the postal code

Hours of Operation: Although the two film sites are not public areas, they are outdoors and can be photographed from close-by at any time, on any day.

Visit Time: You'll need no more than 30 minutes to snap film site reproduction pix after arriving here. However, we highly recommend scheduling 2 to 6 hours in Steveston so that you can enjoy its many *other* fabulous sights and activities.

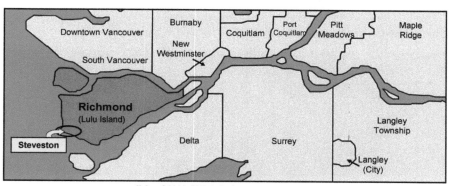

[Map ©2009 GVRD-Richmond (enhanced)]

Considered part of Metro Vancouver, the suburb of **Richmond** is located on **Lulu Island**, which lies just south of South Vancouver. **Steveston Village** is an historic salmon canning community found on the southwestern tip.

[Eclipse screenshot (enhanced)]

Eclipse scenes of Riley leaving Seattle's Pike pub, and the initial bash-and-dash stages of Victoria's attack, were filmed in **Gastown** (Site #31), an historic downtown Vancouver area. In a last ditch effort to escape whatever was attacking him, Riley ran into the mouth of a Gastown alley and was movie-magically transported to a lane between two buildings found at the **Gulf of Georgia Cannery National Historic Site** in Steveston Village.

[Eclipse screenshot (enhanced)]

The boat seen at the end of the alley/lane was moored at the Cannery's dock.

[Eclipse screenshot (enhanced)]

It was on this dock that Victoria finally administered the fateful bite, causing Riley to writhe in agony as her venom began to course through his veins, transforming him into a vampire.

That's *IT* for the Twilight screenshot reproduction opportunities available in Steveston! This film site would receive our **Skip It** rating, were it not for all the other terrific tourist opportunities found in Steveston Village— including some additional film sites that may be of interest.

കൗ

[Steveston Cannery Café ©2012 Dona Janke] [*Once Upon a Time* Granny's Diner screenshot segment]

Once Upon a Time Film Sites

http://onceuponatime.wikia.com/wiki/Steveston_Village
http://www.imdb.com/title/tt1843230/?ref_=nv_sr_1
http://abc.go.com/shows/once-upon-a-time
https://www.facebook.com/OnceABC

From the Tourism Richmond website:

> "There's something enchanted about Richmond's village of Steveston, and if you're a fan of ABC's '*Once Upon a Time*,' you already know this. That's because locations for the TV show's loveable town of Storybrooke—the library, Granny's Diner, Mr. Gold's Pawn Shop and more—are actually shot right here in Steveston!
>
> And while Storybrooke is fiction, Steveston really is a fairytale come to life, with hidden wonder tucked inside hundred-year-old buildings and a magical story all its own! Discover this alluring seaside mix of historic sites, delicious dining and charming shops that together make up one of British Columbia's most beloved destinations."

http://www.tourismrichmond.com/things-to-do/steveston/
http://www.tourismrichmond.com/things-to-do/once/

Storybrooke film sites are not included on our Steveston Twilight Saga Map. Twilighters who also are Once-Upon-a-Timers will find detailed maps of the Storybrooke locations here:
http://www.onceuponatimepodcast.com/ouat-moncton-streetstorybrooke-store-list/

Please Note: If that webpage ever disappears from the Internet, let us know! We captured its info in March of 2015 and can post it as a PDF on the TTTS website.

[Google Maps segments (married & enhanced), ©2015 Google]
http://www.TourTheTwilightSaga.com/B2/VBCtsMaps.pdf

Our **Steveston Twilight Saga Map** identifies all the places discussed in this chapter and will help you follow our Finding the Film Site directions. This map is included in the **Vancouver, BC Twilight Saga Maps PDF** freely posted on our website.

The Steveston Twilight Saga Map Key

FS1: The *Eclipse* Alley/Lane film site

FS2: The *Eclipse* Dock film site

A: Steveston Parking Lot #1

B: Gulf of Georgia Cannery main entrance

C: Steveston Hotel, Café, ATM, Liquor Store, Buck & Ear Pub

D: Fishermen's Car Park (reserved = do not park here)

E: Fisherman's Warf entrance

F: Vancouver Whale Watch office

G: Seabreeze Adventures office and dock

H: Waterfront Boardwalk entrance

I: Britannia Shipyards National Historic Site

J: Steveston Eco Tours dock

K: Steveston Community Centre (Salmon Festival Site)

[©2013 CD Miller]

The Gulf of Georgia Cannery
http://gulfofgeorgiacannery.org/
http://www.pc.gc.ca/lhn-nhs/bc/georgia/index.aspx

Google Maps & SatNav/GPS: 12138 Fourth Ave, Richmond, British Columbia V7E—do not add 3T4 to the postal code

Steveston Twilight Saga Map: Point B

Hours of Operation: 10am to 5pm, 7 days a week—except for October 12th (Canada's Thanksgiving Day); November 11th (Remembrance Day); December 24th, 25th, and 26th (Christmas holiday).

2015 Admission: Adults $7.80, Seniors (65+) $6.55, Youths (6-16 y/o) $3.90, Children under 6 free.

Built in 1894, the Gulf of Georgia Cannery is the largest building of its kind and once was the leading canned salmon producer in British Columbia. Today, as one of BC's few historically intact canneries, it has become a marvelous museum that commemorates the rich history of Canada's West Coast fishing industry.

> "Inside the massive wooden building visitors will experience an introductory film, guided tours with knowledgeable interpreters, and interactive exhibits. This vibrant heritage is justly celebrated in the picturesque fishing village of Steveston, home to Canada's largest fishing fleet as well as many tempting shops and restaurants."

Several special events and exhibits are offered here throughout the year. Visit the Cannery's website to learn what's available during your visit.
http://gulfofgeorgiacannery.org/visit/whats-on

Highlights from the Cannery's 2015 Schedule:
From October (2014) to April, an indoor **Farmer's Market** is hosted by the Cannery on every other Sunday—open from 10am to 3pm.

> "Continuing the tradition of the Steveston winter farmers' market as a local attraction and a gathering place for hundreds of neighbors, the market provides an opportunity for farmers and artisans to showcase their products. Our vendors adhere to the 'Make it, Bake it, Grow it, Catch it' philosophy. Only approved products that are made, baked, grown, raised, caught or harvested by approved B.C. vendors can be sold."

> http://gulfofgeorgiacannery.org/farmers-market

Between May and October, the **Steveston Community Society** holds their **Farmers and Artisans Market** in the area outside the Cannery on two Sundays each month—3 Sundays in August—open from 10am to 4pm.
http://sfam.ca/
https://www.facebook.com/StevestonFarmersandArtisansMarket

If you visit on **Canada Day**—July 1st—Gulf of Georgia Cannery museum admission is free. Although you'll encounter quite a crowd on Canada Day,

the several **Steveston Salmon Festival** activities offered elsewhere will keep you entertained for hours! (More Salmon Festival info below.)
http://gulfofgeorgiacannery.org/events/canada-day

On Friday evenings in July and August, the Cannery hosts an **Outdoor Summer Concert Series**.

> "A wide range of musical tastes will be represented. Admission by donation ($5 and up)."
>
> http://gulfofgeorgiacannery.org/events/music-at-the-cannery

The **Best Catch Sustainable Seafood Festival** is hosted by the Cannery each year, on a Sunday in September.

> "The festival will help you to discover which seafood choices are best for the planet, while cooking demonstrations by famous local chefs will show you which are most delicious! After visiting 'Best Catch' stroll down to the public wharf and pick up some fresh seafood and try one of the demonstration recipes when you get home."
>
> http://gulfofgeorgiacannery.org/events/best-catch-sustainable-seafood-festival
> http://bestcatch.gulfofgeorgiacannery.org/

Please Note: In 2015, the Cannery's Best Catch festival date is September 13th—the last day of the **Forever Twilight in Forks** Stephenie Meyer Days celebration in Forks, Washington (TTTS Book 1, Site #4). If you're willing to skip the Sunday SMD activities, leave Forks early in the morning and go to Steveston, you can enjoy both.
http://forkswa.com/forevertwilightinforks/
https://www.facebook.com/smdforks

[©2013 CD Miller]

The Steveston Hotel—and Much, Much More
http://www.thesteveston.com

Google Maps & SatNav/GPS: 12111 Third Ave, Richmond, BC V7E 3K1

Steveston Twilight Saga Map: Point C

There appears to be only one "hotel" in the village, and this is it.

> "Formerly the Sockeye Hotel, The Steveston Hotel was established in 1895 at the corner of 3rd Avenue and Moncton in the village of Steveston. The Hotel has always been a popular meeting place for the local residents, fishermen and visitors. The Steveston Hotel has had a very colorful past. In July 1900, during the fishing strike, the hotel was home to the Duke of Connaught's troops and is one of the few buildings to survive the fire of May 1918."

Only a few steps away from the Gulf of Georgia Cannery, the Steveston Hotel has far more to offer than quaintly historic (and reasonably-priced) lodgings.

The Steveston Hotel Café is open daily from 7:30am to 2pm (until 3pm on Saturdays and Sundays), closed only on a few major Canadian holidays. In addition to well-prepared, standard breakfast and lunch fare, the Steveston Café offers delicious *salmon* Fish & Chips—something CD Miller had never heard of before thoroughly enjoying it here.

Gordon P, a TripAdvisor reviewer, visited in January of 2015 and had this to say about the Steveston Hotel Café:

> "We joined my sister and brother in law for breakfast. ... [and] walked into a piece of Steveston history. Old style décor, I envision the fishermen sharing tales of their daily successes or not. A stroll thru historical Steveston should include a stop here. The Steveston Café has great atmosphere, delicious food and a staff that is long term and dedicated to your enjoyment and satisfaction. Local or visitor, go there! I have been back again since the first visit and it is honest, true and real in every aspect of the word."
>
> http://www.tripadvisor.com/Restaurant_Review-g181716-d3822871-Reviews-The_ Steveston_Cafe_Hotel-Richmond_British_Columbia.html

But wait, there's more! You'll find an ATM here, and a **Liquor Store** (including beer and wine) that is open every day from 9am to 11pm. And then, there's the Steveston Hotel's **Buck & Ear Bar and Grill:**

"The Buck & Ear Bar and Grill boasts a 350 seat pub with two patios for your enjoyment. Our menu features the best selection of appies, pizzas, burgers, sandwiches and entrees to satisfy even the pickiest of taste buds."

http://www.thesteveston.com/Buck/

Featuring live music from 10pm to 2am on Saturdays and Sundays, the Buck & Ear has Karaoke on most weekdays. On Wednesdays, Rachael Chatoor—a well-known Vancouver musician—performs acoustic sets all day.
http://rachaelchatoor.com/

Buck & Ear Hours of Operation: Monday to Wednesday, 11am-Midnight; Thursday, 11am-1:00am; Friday & Saturday, Noon-2am; Sunday, 10 am-Midnight.

[©2014 StevestonLife film site location segment (enhanced)]

Lastly, for Once-Upon-a-Timer-Twilighters: the Steveston Hotel's main entrance has occasionally been seen as the **Storybrooke Liquor Store**.

The Steveston Fisherman's Wharf & Floating Fish Market

Google Maps & SatNav/GPS: 3800 Bayview Street, Steveston, BC

Steveston Twilight Saga Map: Point E

Fish Market Hours of Operation: Seven days a week, from approximately 8am to 5pm. The time varies with each fisher, as well as weather conditions, with more fishers usually present on Fridays through Sundays than on weekdays.

Fisherman's Wharf is one of the most picturesque and entertaining places in all of Steveston, and its entrance is only 3 blocks away from the Gulf of Georgia Cannery. Every Steveston business listed with a 3800 Bayview Street address is in the Fisherman's Wharf area.
http://www.stevestonivillage.com/stevestongiftandsouvenirshops.html

[©2014 http://www.hayleyonholiday.com] [©2012 http://www.girlsgoneawhile.com]

On your way to the actual wharf after entering at Point E, you'll encounter several souvenir and gift shops; clothing stores and boutiques; cafés, coffee houses, and sweet shops.

[©2013 http://www.rtwgirl.com]

When you reach the wharf that stretches out into Steveston Harbor, you'll find the floating Fish Market. Here you can buy seafood that's *literally* fresh off the ship—the fishmongers who operate here sell directly from their boats!

[©2013 http://www.rtwgirl.com] [©2011 http://yeogolf.blogspot.com]

Freshly caught (or freshly frozen-at-sea) prawns, shrimp, sardines, halibut, cod, tuna, and many other types of seasonal seafood are available here, at amazingly low prices.

Even if your lodgings don't afford you the ability to cook, strolling through the floating fish market is an experience you'll not want to miss.

From the Steveston Fish Market website:

- Great views of the river, harbor and Steveston Landing
- Photo opportunities at every turn
- Music by talented local musicians on Steveston Landing
- Ready-to-eat food and refreshments onshore
- Lots of fresh-off-the-ocean sea breezes
- Great people watching of residents and visitors from around the world
- Miscellaneous entertainment throughout the season

http://www.stevestonivillage.com/stevestonfishmarket.html

[©2015 Vancouver Aquarium segment (enhanced): "Newborn killer whales spotted off BC coast."]

Whale Watching Excursions

If you've ever been interested in getting up close and personal with whales, Vancouver is one of the best places to do so.

From Tourism Vancouver:

"Each year from March to October, thousands of whales migrate through the waters near Vancouver, making it one of the world's best locations for prime whale watching. … Many varieties of whales pass through these northern waterways, including humpback whales, orcas ['killer whales'], gray whales and minke whales. …

The waters around Vancouver Island host large resident pods of nearly 100 killer whales, as well as small pods of transient orcas …

From sea lions and otters to dolphins and birds, British Columbia's remote coastal areas are rife with a wide range of marine creatures. Keep an eye out—and your camera ready."

http://www.tourismvancouver.com/do/activities-attractions/whale-watching/

Vancouver boasts *numerous* whale watching tour companies, and three of them operate out of Steveston.

Vancouver Whale Watch (Map Point F)
http://www.vancouverwhalewatch.com

Seabreeze Adventures (Map Point G)
http://www.seabreezeadventures.ca/

Steveston Eco Tours (Map Point J)
http://www.stevestonecotours.ca/

To assist you in researching Steveston's whale watching tour companies, we've created a **Comparison Table** based on information available in March of 2015.
http://www.TourTheTwilightSaga.com/B2/WhaleWatchingComparisonTable.pdf

[©2007 O B JoshK] [©2014 Cascadia Girl]

Britannia Shipyards National Historic Site

http://britannia-hss.ca/
http://www.richmond.ca/culture/sites/britannia/about.htm

Google Maps & SatNav/GPS: 5180 Westwater Drive, Richmond BC, V7E 6P3

Steveston Twilight Saga Map: Point I

Hours of Operation: Open Saturdays and Sundays from October to April, 12pm-5pm, with special opening hours during spring break in March; From May to September, open 7 days a week, 10am-5pm.

Admission: Free for all ages—Donations greatly appreciated

Please Note: Although parking is free at Britannia Shipyards' two small car parks, each has a 3-hour limit. You might want to park in the *Eclipse* film sites' lot (Steveston Twilight Saga Map Point A), pay for 6 hours of parking, and walk to Britannia Shipyards after enjoying other Steveston Village tourist attractions.

From the Britannia Shipyards website:

"Britannia is a rare example of the type of village which once served the thriving fishing industry with its canneries, boatyards, stores, homes and its mix of cultures. This national historic site is representative of the diverse community built on pilings and connected by boardwalks."

From Richmond's website:

"The Britannia Shipyards National Historic Site is an authentic representation of a once thriving community of canneries, boat yards, residences and stores. ...

Tour the oldest shipyard buildings in British Columbia and observe ongoing boat restoration projects as you experience a bygone time when fishing and boatbuilding were flourishing industries on the Fraser River.

Many of the buildings date back to 1885 and tell the stories of multi-ethnic residents and workers at the Britannia Cannery and Britannia Shipyard: Chinese, European, First Nations and Japanese."

[©2012 Kate Bagnall] [©2011 Tom McGregor]

Go to the Richmond website to learn more about the many historic buildings and demonstrations that can be enjoyed at the Britannia Shipyards. You'll also find a **Britannia Site Map** link on that page.
http://www.richmond.ca/culture/sites/britannia/site.htm

[Bing Bird's Eye Map segments (married & enhanced), ©2015 Microsoft Corp.]

Please Note: The Britannia Shipyards (Point I) and Steveston Eco Tours dock (Point J) are only a 15 minute walk from Fisherman's Warf, if you follow the **Waterfront Boardwalk**. Point H on the Steveston Twilight Saga Map marks the boardwalk's entrance, found just past the can't-miss-it orca statue flying above the entrance to Seabreeze Adventures' dock (Point G).

Follow the Waterfront Boardwalk southeast, cross the bridge at the mouth of the Imperial Landing Park inlet, and keep heading southeast (following the shore) until you reach Britannia Shipyards.

[© Steveston Salmon Festival] [© Steveston Salmon Festival, SandraSteier.com]

The Steveston Salmon Festival
http://www.stevestonsalmonfest.ca/
https://www.facebook.com/StevestonSalmonFestival

Google Maps & SatNav/GPS: 4111 Moncton Street Richmond, B.C., V7E 3A8

Steveston Twilight Saga Map: Point K

July 1st, from 6:30am-5pm

Admission: The parade, performances, activities and demonstrations, are free.

If the dates of your Vancouver visit include **Canada Day** (July 1st), you'll encounter huge crowds of people celebrating Canada's birthday almost anywhere you go on that day, making it difficult to snap screenshot reproduction pix at any of the metropolitan Vancouver film sites.
http://en.wikipedia.org/wiki/Canada_Day

Considering the meager *Eclipse* screenshot opportunities available at the Gulf of Georgia Cannery on *any* day, we strongly suggest that you visit Steveston on Canada Day, so that you can enjoy the fabulous **Steveston Salmon Festival**.

"The people of Steveston have come together every year since 1945 to celebrate Canada's birthday and the rich heritage of our community.

The day begins at 10am with a parade through historic Steveston village, which features over 100 entries. Then, the [Steveston Salmon] Festival is officially kicked off at our Opening Ceremonies on the Main Stage at noon with the singing of *O Canada*. After the official opening, the stage bursts with great entertainment all afternoon. Festival highlights include attractions such as the Japanese Cultural Show, Craft Fair, Trade Show, an awesome Children's Festival, Martial Arts Demonstrations, Youth Rock Fest, Food Fair plus an Art Show & Exhibit.

The main attraction is our famous salmon barbecue where over 1200 pounds of wild salmon filets are grilled over open fire pits. This popular treat sells out every year! $15 per plate, cash only.

Whatever your age, whatever your interests, there is something for everyone at the Steveston Salmon Festival!"

[© Steveston Salmon Festival] [© Steveston Salmon Festival, SandraSteier.com]

The Steveston Salmon Festival will mark its 70th anniversary in 2015, and we're sure that they'll plan extraordinary events for this platinum occasion. Below is the 2014 schedule events, to give you an idea of what is offered.

6:30am - 11:30am - Pancake Breakfast (hosted by 12th Richmond Scouts, located in the 'Food Fair' in the parking lot at the Steveston Community Centre) $8 per plate, cash only

8:30am - Citizenship Ceremony - Main Stage

9:30am - Kid's Bicycle Parade

10:00am - noon - Canada Day Parade

Noon - Opening Ceremony

10:00am - 5:00pm - various locations - Japanese Cultural Displays, Martial Arts Demos, Art Show, Children's Festival, Craft Fair, Trade Show, Food Fair, Community Information Tables, Salmon Festival Car Show

11:00am until sold out - Salmon Barbecue $15 per plate (CASH ONLY)

12:00pm - 5:00pm - Horticulture Show, Youth Rock Fest

[©2007 Arnold C]

Though only a small fishing village, the sights and activities discussed above are merely the iceberg-tip of Steveston's tourist attractions. To learn about the many other attractions available here, go to:
http://www.steveston.bc.ca/activities.html
http://www.stevestonivillage.com/stevestonthingstodo.html

You'll also encounter an avalanche of amazing eateries when visiting Steveston. Check them out ahead of time at:
http://www.tourismrichmond.com/restaurants/-steveston/

Going to Steveston

 ### Via Public Transportation

Visit the Steveston Village website for public transportation directions.
http://www.steveston.bc.ca/directions.html

Please Note: A Shuttle Bus to Steveston from several Vancouver and Richmond hotels ($15 round-trip) is available if you book a tour with Vancouver Whale Watch or Seabreeze Adventures.
http://www.vancouverwhalewatch.com/shuttle.html
http://www.seabreezeadventures.ca/shuttle/

🚗 Via Automobile

Google Maps & SatNav/GPS: 12138 Fourth Ave, Richmond, British
  Columbia V7E—do not add 3T4 to the postal code

The coordinates above will lead you to the largest Steveston car park—
Parking Lot #1—only a few steps away from the Gulf of Georgia Cannery
and the two *Eclipse* film sites.

- Park in an available stall and note the number
- Enter your stall number at the pay station
- Select the amount of time you wish to park*
- Pay by credit card or exact coins
- Collect receipt
- There is no need to display the receipt

Parking proceeds support the Gulf of Georgia Cannery National Historic
Site.

*Staying longer than the time you paid for may result in a $70 parking
violation. Purchase more time than you think you'll need, or be sure to pop
back and buy more time before it expires.

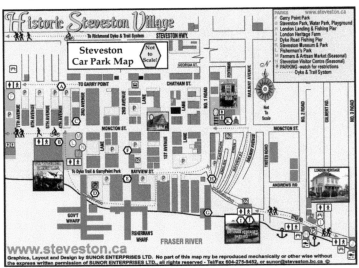

[©Sunor Enterprises LTD (enhanced), http://www.steveston.bc.ca/map.html]
http://www.TourTheTwilightSaga.com/B2/VBCtsMaps.pdf

In our Vancouver, BC Twilight Saga Maps PDF you'll find a **Steveston Car
Park Map** that shows other public parking places in the village. Because that
map is not to scale, we've added Steveston Twilight Saga Map identifiers to

it, to help you recognize where each car park is in relationship to where you might be heading.

Please Note: Most car parks within the village have a 3-hour time limit. Be sure to follow the pay station directions—some lots may be pay-and-*display*.

⊂ଃ৪ଠ

[©2013 CD Miller]

Finding the Film Sites

At the south end of Parking Lot #1 you'll see a large Gulf of Georgia Cannery National Historic Site sign. Go to the sidewalk that runs behind that sign and turn right (west). When you reach the lane between the Cannery's building and its neighbor, you'll be at the entrance to the *Eclipse* Alley/Lane film site: **FS1** on the Steveston Twilight Saga Map.

[Eclipse Special Features screenshot segment (enhanced)]

This lane is private property. The neighboring building belongs to the Steveston Harbor Authority and the lane is part of a working dock. Thus, the access gate may be closed.

[©2013 CD Miller]

When visiting very early on a Thursday in September of 2013, CD Miller found the lane wide open. Instead of walking into it, however, Miller snapped pix from the entrance. The photo above is the central segment of a pic she shot from that viewpoint—and it looks just like the Special Features screenshot above.

Thus, you'll be able to snap *Eclipse* Alley/Lane screenshot reproduction pix even if the lane's gate is closed. Just be sure that your camera is set to snap high-resolution photos, so that when you crop them down to the central segment they'll still look crystal clear.

When finished at the Alley/Lane film site, return to the sidewalk and head back the way you came (east), passing the sign, until you can turn right and follow the fish!

[©2013 CD Miller]

The fish embedded in the path will lead you to the Gulf of Georgia Cannery's main entrance. (Miller visited before 10am, when the museum was open.)

The *Eclipse* Dock film site (**FS2** on the Steveston Twilight Saga Map) is also a working dock and private property. To actually step on it without trespassing, you must pay to go through the Cannery. They have arranged to include a small area of the dock as part of their museum attractions.

[Eclipse screenshot (enhanced)]

[©2013 CD Miller]

Happily, Twilighters who don't have time to tour the Cannery's museum—or Twilighters who aren't interested in touring it—can shoot *Eclipse* Dock film site *Special Features* screenshot reproductions from a neighboring dock, reached via the reserved Fishermen's Car Park (Point D).

[©2013 CD Miller]

From the Cannery's main entrance, continue walking southeast until you've passed the public toilets (seen above), then turn right. Follow the curving westside drive of the Fishermen's Car Park until you reach the neighboring dock. The Special Features screenshot below was shot from that dock.

[Eclipse Special Features screenshot (enhanced)]

[©2013 CD Miller]

Because it's a working dock, there's sure to be one or more picturesque fishing boats moored there. Unfortunately, there also may be one or more automobiles parked on the dock.

When finished shooting your *Eclipse* Dock film site pix, you can head back to the car park, leave Steveston, and proceed to your next Twilight Saga destination.

   Or, you can return to the Fishermen's Car Park entrance, turn right, and walk southeast on Bayview Street to enjoy other Steveston Village sights and attractions.

Pemberton, British Columbia
The Denali Coven Home
A *Breaking Dawn* Part 2 Film Site

Google Maps & SatNav/GPS: 1777 Pinewood Drive, Mount Currie, BC
V0N 2K0

This Film Site is a Private Residence: There are no "Hours of Operation"

Visit Time: 15 minutes is more than enough time to politely snap a few pix
before quietly going away.

[Promotional photo obtained from http://twifan.wikia.com/wiki/Denali_Coven]

The **Denali Coven** is one of only two known "vegetarian" vampire families in the world—the other being the Cullen family. Their name derives from the **Denali** area of the US state of **Alaska**, where they live.
http://twilightsaga.wikia.com/wiki/Denali_coven

Denali is the native name for **Mount McKinley**, an Alaskan mountain that is the highest point in North America.
http://en.wikipedia.org/wiki/Mount_McKinley

Owned by the US federal government, **Denali National Park and Preserve** encompasses over 6 million acres of land in the Alaskan interior, with Denali/Mount McKinley at its center.
http://www.nps.gov/dena/index.htm
http://en.wikipedia.org/wiki/Denali_National_Park_and_Preserve

Because there are no dwellings within Denali National Park and Preserve, we presume that the coven's home is located somewhere in **Denali Borough**.
http://www.denaliborough.govoffice.com/
http://en.wikipedia.org/wiki/Denali_Borough,_Alaska

That said, no Twilight Saga movie scenes were filmed in Alaska!

[Breaking Dawn Part 2 screenshot segment (enhanced)]

The real-world structure used to shoot *Breaking Dawn* Part 2 scenes of Renesmee's introduction to the Denali Coven is located on the outskirts of **Pemberton, British Columbia**.
http://www.pemberton.ca/; http://www.tourismpembertonbc.com/
http://en.wikipedia.org/wiki/Pemberton,_British_Columbia

[©2013 CD Miller]

This Home is a Private Residence!

If you come here, please abide by the **Twilighter Treaty**, so that others can continue to enjoy this site long after you've gone.

Do not trespass on private property.
Do not disturb—or photograph—the residents.
Do not bite any humans, for any reason.

[©2013 http://www.photosbyshew.com]

The Pemberton film site is assigned a Might-be-Fun rating because:

- In relationship to what little can be photographed here *Twilight*-wise, the time required to visit Pemberton is excessive, thus it ought to be a **Skip It** site.
  However …
- The scenery enjoyed during the 5 hour (round-trip) drive between Vancouver and Pemberton is stunning, awesome, gorgeous, magnificent!
- A wide variety of terrific non-Twilight tourist attractions lie along the route.
- Twihards divinely inspired to visit every recognizable film site, and Twilighters with tons of holiday time, will thoroughly enjoy devoting an entire day to this trip.

Please Note: Being a remote mountain location, both grizzly and black bears freely roam the Pemberton area, as do cougars, lynx, bobcats, wolves, coyotes, foxes, and wolverines. Review the **Wildlife Warnings** appendix at the back of this book during your drive.

∽ℭℬ℘℩

[Bing map segments (married & enhanced), ©2015 Nokia/Microsoft Corp]

Going to Pemberton

🚆 Via Public Transportation

http://www.pembertonchamber.com/pemberton/resources/transportation/
http://www.seatosky.worldweb.com/Pemberton/Transportation/Taxis/

Pemberton is not easily accessible via public transportation. The film site is about an hour's hike (one-way) from the Pemberton Greyhound bus station. If you must use public transportation to get here, consider pre-booking a taxi from Pemberton's only cab company to reach the film site.

🚗 Via Automobile

Google Maps & SatNav/GPS: 1777 Pinewood Drive, Mount Currie, BC
V0N 2K0

Pemberton is a 2.5 hour drive north of Vancouver, along Highway 99—the **Sea-To-Sky Highway**—5 hours round-trip. Inclement weather or highway repair activities may increase the drive time by an hour or more.
http://en.wikipedia.org/wiki/British_Columbia_Highway_99

Please Note: It is well worth the effort to get an early start—6am—to avoid the *horrendously congested* Vancouver rush hour traffic between 7 and 9am.

[©2014 Gemma & JR http://offtracktravel.ca/]

Driving to and from the Pemberton Film Site

As we mentioned before, the Sea-to-Sky highway journey between Vancouver and Pemberton is phenomenally scenic.
http://www.infovancouver.com/excursions/sea-to-sky-highway

> "The Sea to Sky Highway is frequently rated up there as one of the most beautiful stretches of road in the world. Hugging the coast all the way to the top of Howe Sound, then heading inland, you are guaranteed some spectacular scenery along the way and a number of scenic viewpoints where you can stop and safely enjoy the views."

Below are a few of the many non-*Twilight* attractions that can be enjoyed while driving *to* Pemberton.

Cultural Journey Kiosks
http://slcc.ca/experience/cultural-journey/
http://slcc.ca/wp-content/themes/SLCC/library/images/CJ_Map.PDF

Seven cultural information kiosks are found along the Sea-to-Sky Highway. They celebrate the **Squamish** and **Lil'wat** First Nations people indigenous to this area of British Columbia. The Squamish and Lil'wat are considered members of the **Coast Salish** peoples, a group of ethnically- and linguistically-related tribes who have populated the Pacific Northwest Coast for thousands of years—including areas of Washington and Oregon.
http://en.wikipedia.org/wiki/Squamish_Nation
http://en.wikipedia.org/wiki/Lil%27wat_First_Nation
http://en.wikipedia.org/wiki/Indigenous_peoples_of_the_Pacific_Northwest_Coast

Because their language developed independently from Salish, the Quileute are not considered Coast Salish peoples. Shared cultures such as totem carving and canoe building, however, often bring them together.
https://www.pinterest.com/pin/245657354648198342/

149

[©2010 Thomas McIlwraith; Tantalus Lookout Kiosk #6]
http://www.anthroblog.tadmcilwraith.com/2010/04/30/sea-to-sky-cultural-journey/

All of the kiosks are covered by a roof designed in the style of the Coast Salish peoples' woven cedar bark hat. Each has four displays. Two describe the Sea-to-Sky cultural journey and the Squamish Lil'wat Cultural Centre in Whistler. The other two displays are devoted to each site's history and mythology, archaeology, traditional and contemporary Squamish and Lil'wat culture.

Kiosks #1 through #5 are on the east side of the highway. Kiosks #1, #2, and #3 are accessible only from the north-bound lanes—while driving *to* Pemberton. Kiosks #4 and #5 can be reached from either direction of travel. We suggest visiting them while driving back to Vancouver.

Kiosks #6 and #7 are on the west side of the Sea-to-Sky and are accessible only from the south-bound lanes—while driving back to Vancouver.

Unfortunately, the highway signs heralding an upcoming kiosk exit are quite small and easily missed. Furthermore, although Thomas McIlwraith's Sea-to-Sky Cultural Journey website provides an excellent pictorial preview of each kiosk, there doesn't seem to be an online resource that identifies their specific locations. We had to search Google Streetview for hours to find coordinates for each kiosk—but, we did.

[©2010 Thomas McIlwraith]

Horseshoe Bay Kiosk #1

Google Maps SatNav/GPS: 49.364006, -123.273762
https://www.flickr.com/photos/tfm/sets/72157623964186342/detail/

The first kiosk encountered when driving from Vancouver to Pemberton is outside Horseshoe Bay. Its pullover is found just after keeping left to begin traveling north on the Sea-to-Sky highway. (Keeping right takes you into Horseshoe Bay Village and leads to the western end of Trans-Canada Highway 1/North 101 Highway.)

We strongly suggest stopping at Kiosk #1. If you enjoy it, you'll know to visit all of the other kiosks. If it's not your cup of tea, however, drive directly to Pemberton—stopping only at **Kiosk #3** (we'll explain why shortly).

Approximately 30 minutes north of Kiosk #1 you'll see the Sea to Sky Gondola on your right.

The Sea to Sky Gondola

Google Maps SatNav/GPS: 49.674873, -123.158575
http://www.seatoskygondola.com/
https://www.facebook.com/SeaToSkyGondola

> "Tickets include 1 round-trip ride to the summit [12 minutes each way] where you can access the interpretive loop trails, take an informative trail tour, grab a snack at the Summit Lodge while enjoying beautiful views, access vast climbing and hiking trail networks, or walk across the [100-metre-high] Sky Pilot Suspension Bridge to the Spirit Viewing Platform."

The next right turn north of the Sea to Sky Gondola is the exit to Stawamus Chief Provincial Park and Britannia Beach Kiosk #2.

Stawamus Chief Provincial Park

Britannia Beach Kiosk #2

Google Maps SatNav/GPS: 49.678244, -123.156543
http://www.env.gov.bc.ca/bcparks/explore/parkpgs/stawamus/
https://www.flickr.com/photos/tfm/sets/72157623964263016/detail/

Exit from the highway and follow the road as it curves north. Use the round-about to turn left and enter the car park next to a picnic area containing Kiosk #2. When ready to leave, you can reach Kiosk #3 by continuing on the road leading north from the car park.

If you skip Kiosk #2, take the *next* right turn after Stawamus Chief Provincial Park's entrance to reach Kiosk #3.

[©2010 Thomas McIlwraith]

Stawamus Chief Kiosk #3

Google Maps SatNav/GPS: 49.681816, -123.153678
https://www.flickr.com/photos/tfm/sets/72157623964301174/detail/

Kiosk #3 is found at the base of Stawamus Chief, one of the largest granite monoliths in the world. If the background in the photo above looks familiar, it should!

[Breaking Dawn Part 2 screenshot (enhanced)]

The face of Stawamus Chief was seen on screen in scenes of Bella's first hunt as a newborn vampire. According to Twilight Girl Forever in Portland:

> "The [Stawamus Chief] rock face was used in Breaking Dawn
> Part 2 when Bella smelled the guy climbing it and took off running
> after him. ...

I am not sure how much of the scene was real or done with a green screen. The rock face is huge and stands tall above the river. It definitely made for a realistic background view for the movie."

http://twilightgirlportland.com/bd-2-movie-location-stawamus-chief-rock-face/

We're saving Kiosks #4 and #5 for our driving directions back to Vancouver from Pemberton. When you're done at Kiosk #3, get back on the Sea-to-Sky and drive the remaining 1 hour and 12 minutes north to Pemberton.

C3&O

Upon entering Pemberton, you'll have reached the end of the Sea-to-Sky Highway. Highway 99, however, continues east and becomes Portage Road. Stay on it. After passing the McDonald's, watch on your right for the Pemberton Valley Lodge.

[©2013 CD Miller]

Pemberton Valley Lodge

Google Maps & SatNav/GPS: 50.315079,-122.792798
http://www.pembertonvalleylodge.com/

Many 2011 Twi-fan articles reported that *Breaking Dawn* filming took place *at* the lodge. It didn't. This is, however, where the cast stayed during Pemberton filming.
http://hollywoodlife.com/pics/robert-pattinson-kristen-stewart-breaking-dawn-filming-vancouver-pemberton-lodge/

Stop for a fresh-roasted cup of Starbucks coffee in the lodge's lobby on your way to the film site—or on your way back. The first turn leading to the film site is approximately 2 minutes east of the lodge's driveway.

[Google Maps segment (enhanced), ©2013 Google]

Finding the Film Site

Google Maps & SatNav/GPS: 1777 Pinewood Drive, Mount Currie, BC
VON 2K0

After crossing the Lillooet River, watch for **Pemberton Farm Road East**, and turn left. Take the next right onto **Pinewood Drive**.

Pinewood Drive winds its way through a small community of private residences, heading uphill. Stay on it, passing Pemberton Plateau road on your left ... passing the Pinewood Drive cul-de-sac on your right ... passing the Pinewood Place cul-de-sac on your right ... continuing to wind your way up until you drive around a blind curve to the right and suddenly see the Denali Coven's house perched at the road's end.

[©2013 CD Miller]

Because you just rounded a blind curve, do not stop here. Continue driving toward the house, but turn around just after passing the fire hydrant seen at right, above—*before* reaching the home's driveway—and head back the way you came.

Stop just after returning to the fire hydrant, parking as far right as possible without pulling off the road and damaging the flora. (As seen below, CD Miller parked *at* the curve. In hindsight, we realized that wasn't any safer than parking on the left side after rounding the curve.)

Now you can get out and snap your pix of the house. Avoid trespassing by going no closer than the fire hydrant.

[©2013 CD Miller]

BTW: The reverse view from the Denali Coven house—when facing south from the fire hydrant—is this film site's second screenshot reproduction opportunity. (Another plus for parking at the fire hydrant: your car won't be in the pic, as Miller's is!)

[Breaking Dawn Part 2 screenshot (enhanced)]

Obviously, there will only be snow on the peaks and roadside boulders if you visit during the winter months. Twilighters who enjoy winter sports should consider planning a ski trip to the **Whistler Blackcomb Ski Resort**—36 km (22 mi) south of Pemberton.
http://www.whistlerblackcomb.com/

[©2013 CD Miller]

Spectacular Pemberton valley vistas are visible from the Denali Coven's promontory, however it is best not to tarry too long near private property—especially since there are plenty of things to do elsewhere.

[©2013 Cheryl Young; Nairn Falls] [©2013 Gillian McMillan; The Squamish Lil'wat Cultural Centre]

Driving Back to Vancouver

Below are *some* of the many attractions found south of Pemberton, listed in order of their location on the Sea-to-Sky drive back to Vancouver.

Nairn Falls Provincial Park

Google Maps & SatNav/GPS: 1777 Pinewood Drive, Mount Currie, BC
V0N 2K0
http://en.wikipedia.org/wiki/Nairn_Falls_Provincial_Park
http://www.env.gov.bc.ca/bcparks/explore/parkpgs/nairn_falls/

> "Just ... 5 minutes [south] from Pemberton town center, is Nairn Falls Park. ... The falls are 60 m high and a 1.5 km [just under 1 mile] hiking trail will take you to the viewpoint."

Whistler

Google Maps & SatNav/GPS: Whistler, BC, Canada or 50.122257, -122.960066
http://www.whistler.com/
http://en.wikipedia.org/wiki/Whistler,_British_Columbia

> "Whistler is a Canadian resort town ... During the 2010 Winter Olympics, [Whistler Blackcomb Ski Resort] hosted most of the alpine, Nordic, luge, skeleton, and bobsled events, though freestyle skiing and all snowboarding events were hosted at Cypress Mountain near Vancouver."

Happily, Whistler isn't only a winter fun spot. In fact, a mind-numbing number of activities are available during the spring, summer, and fall. Here are just a *few* of the local attractions listed on Whistler.com:

- The world record-breaking **Peak 2 Peak Gondola** is a breathtaking experience. Spanning the distance between Whistler and Blackcomb mountains, the ride is a 90 minute round-trip and a "special glass-bottom gondola for a bird's-eye view of the forest" is available. If you plan to hike on either peak, or dine at the mountaintop restaurants, you can spend hours enjoying your Peak 2 Peak Gondola ticket.
- Absolutely amazing **Zipline Tours** are available, ranging from 2.5 to 4.5 hours.
- White water rafting (leisurely or challenging), horseback riding, bungee jumping ...
- Hiking, mountain-biking, Scandinavian spa, golf, helicopter tours ... the list goes on and on.

Please Note: Grab a beverage and get comfy before you visit Whistler. com. It takes at least a couple of hours just to explore all the activities and attractions described on their website!

[©2010 Thomas McIlwraith]

The Squamish Lil'wat Cultural Centre in Whistler

Google Maps & SatNav/GPS: 4584 Blackcomb Way, Whistler, BC V0N 1B4
http://slcc.ca/

"Built to preserve their culture and share it with others, the building is designed to evoke the longhouses of the Squamish people and the Istken (traditional earthen pit house) of the Lil'wat people with a modern architectural interpretation. ... The [centre] celebrates the joint history of the Squamish and Lil'wat First Nations, past and present, by showcasing their histories, creative works and cultures in an interactive format. ... The gift shop and café can be accessed without paying the admission fee to the Centre—making it the perfect place in Whistler to pick up a memorable gift."

http://www.anthroblog.tadmcilwraith.com/2010/05/02/skwxwu7mesh-lilwat7ul-cultural-centre/

"The [Squamish Lil'wat Cultural Centre] in Whistler is a fantastic culmination to the Sea-to-Sky Cultural Journey. I arrived at the Centre early on a Wednesday afternoon and was struck immediately by the stunning approaches to the building. Inside, the beauty of the Great Hall was almost overwhelming. The very friendly staff helped me register as a local visitor which, for the price of a one day admission, gives access to the Centre for a year. They also set me up with an iPod-like device so that I could tour the centre with audio accompaniment."

[©2013 Jimmy Abbott: http://www.onelifeonewhistler.com/]

Brandywine Falls & Kiosk #5

Google Maps & SatNav/GPS: 50.037830, -123.122510
http://www.env.gov.bc.ca/bcparks/explore/parkpgs/brandywine_falls/
http://en.wikipedia.org/wiki/Brandywine_Falls_Provincial_Park

The entrance to beautiful Brandywine Falls Provincial Park is located 7 miles (11 km) south of Whistler—approximately a 17 minute drive. The kiosk will be on your left, just before reaching the car park.

From the parking lot, a 40 minute (round-trip) walk through the forest will let you enjoy the closest viewing platform overlooking Brandywine Falls; a spectacular 230 foot (70 metre) waterfall. Those happy for a longer hike can continue to a second Brandywine Falls viewpoint that also offers gorgeous vistas of the surrounding area, including Daisy Lake and the distinctively unusual Black Tusk rock formation.
http://en.wikipedia.org/wiki/The_Black_Tusk

When finished, it's about a 15 minute drive to the next place of interest.

[©2013 CD Miller]

159

Tantalus Lookout & Kiosk #6

Google Maps & SatNav/GPS: 49.847280, -123.150169
http://en.wikipedia.org/wiki/Tantalus_Range
https://www.flickr.com/photos/tfm/sets/72157623964442296/detail/

Whether or not you're interested in Kiosk #6, you must stop at the Tantalus Lookout on your way back to Vancouver. Approximately 25 minutes south of Whistler, this pullover offers particularly stunning views of the Tantalus mountains and the lush valley that stretches between them and the Sea-to-Sky highway.

The next potential stop is 15 minutes' drive further south.

[©2010 Thomas McIlwraith]

The Squamish Adventure Centre & Kiosk #4

Google Maps & SatNav/GPS: 38551 Loggers Lane, Squamish, BC V8B 0H2
http://www.tourismsquamish.com/attractions/squamish-adventure-centre
http://www.adventurecentre.ca/
https://www.facebook.com/SquamishAdventureCentre
https://www.flickr.com/photos/tfm/sets/72157623839927197/

As you can see in the photo above, Kiosk #4 is adjacent to the Squamish Adventure Centre. From the Tourism Squamish website:

> "The Squamish Adventure Centre was developed through a collaborative operating philosophy—one where partners in the building promote their respective sectors throughout Squamish. In this way, the Centre acts as a hub to effectively market all of Squamish. The Squamish Adventure Centre houses:
>
> • Visitor Information
> • Ticket Sales Kiosk

- Activity Booking Desk
- Bike & Paddleboard Rentals
- Café Garibaldi
- The Squamish Store
- Theatre—rotating movie selections
- Squamish Chamber of Commerce"

[©2010 Thomas McIlwraith]

Tunnel Point Kiosk #7

Google Maps & SatNav/GPS: 49.484069, -123.247968
https://www.flickr.com/photos/tfm/sets/72157623964486466/detail/
http://slcc.ca/wp-content/themes/SLCC/library/images/CJ_Map.PDF

The last of the Sea-to-Sky cultural kiosks is located 23 minutes south of the Squamish Adventure Centre. According to the Squamish Lil'wat Cultural Centre's Cultural Journey map, Kiosk #7 lies at:

> "A vantage point to the islands of Howe Sound where mythical serpents and Sasquatches roam, and where Mink and Skunk held their infamous feast. To the north is Porteau Cove, a sturgeon fishing area and one of the oldest archaeological sites on the Northwest coast."

After perusing the Tunnel Point Kiosk display posters, walk the short path found behind the kiosk to reach a remarkable viewpoint that overlooks the mouth of Howe Sound and its islands.

[©2015 http://www.hellobc.com/]

Again, we've only reviewed a few of the many non-*Twilight* tourist attractions that lie along the Sea-to-Sky Highway journey between Vancouver and Pemberton. If you're interested in learning about more of them, visit the websites below.

http://www.hellobc.com/driving-routes/31/sea-to-sky-highway-route.aspx
http://www.infovancouver.com/excursions/sea-to-sky-highway
http://www.lonelyplanet.com/canada/british-columbia/sea-to-sky-highway/things-to-do

36

Whytecliff Park
A *New Moon* Film Site
http://whytecliffpark.com/
http://en.wikipedia.org/wiki/Whytecliff_Park

Google Maps: 49.371229, -123.288996

Hours of Operation: Dawn to dusk

Visit Time: 30 minutes is plenty of time to walk from the closest car park to the film site, snap a few pix, and return to your car.

CB80

[New Moon screenshot (enhanced)]

While driving Jacob and the newly-restored motorcycles to her first lesson, Bella rounds a corner and notices four men rough-housing on the ledge of a cliff across the water. Suddenly, two of them grab another. He struggles, and they toss him off the cliff.

[New Moon screenshot (enhanced)]

Seeing this, Bella slams on the brakes, pulls her truck over and dashes to the edge of the road.

> BELLA
> Oh my God! Stop them!
>
> JACOB
> They're not really fighting, Bella. They're cliff diving.
>
> BELLA
> What, on purpose?
>
> JACOB
> Scary as hell, but a total rush.

[©2013 CD Miller]

All of the roadside footage for these scenes was filmed on a Marine Drive curve, just before reaching **Whytecliff Park**. The cliff where Sam's pack is seen, however, was digitally created by special effects teams.

[New Moon screenshot (enhanced)]

According to an interview published by Bill Desowitz in 2009:

"For the cliff scenes, [**Prime Focus' Digital Matte Painting department in LA**] designed the entire landscape using several locations in Vancouver's Whytecliff Park as reference. The team also provided on-set vfx supervision for … a greenscreen shoot at Vancouver Film Studios of a stuntman jumping 70 feet off a tower as a camera rig does a 270-degree tilt, following him from the top of the cliff until he hits water."

http://www.awn.com/articles/article/new-moon-twilight/page/2,1

[©2013 CD Miller]

Above is the real-world view from the point where Bella parked her truck.

Whytecliff Park is Assigned a Skip It Rating Because:

Although you'll recognize the stretch of road and layby where Bella pulled over, your time would be much better spent visiting other—far more Twilicious—Vancouver film sites.

That said, Twihards divinely inspired to visit every film site can drive to Whytecliff Park from **Stanley Park** (Site #32) in only 25 minutes.

If you'll be going to **Pemberton** (Site #35), you can make a quick Whytecliff Park stop at the beginning or end of your day. It is reached from Highway 99 (Trans-Canada Highway 1) in West Vancouver, approximately 6 minutes before entering—or 6 minutes after leaving—the Sea-To-Sky Highway.

[Google Maps segment (enhanced), ©2015 Google]

Going to the Whytecliff Park Film Site

Google Maps & SatNav/GPS: 7120 Marine Drive, West Vancouver, BC V7W 2T4

Unless you're driving a truck that looks like Bella's, do *not* park in the pullout used for filming. Stopping on a blind curve is a serious safety risk.

Instead, drive past the film site and park in the closest section of the Whytecliff Park parking lot. The film site is only about a 5 minute walk away. Follow the ocean-side of the road until you see Bella's pullout, then snap your pix and head back to your car.

Should you need them, public toilets are available at Whytecliff Park.

37

Vancouver Island

New Moon & *Breaking Dawn* Beach Film Sites

Google Maps: Vancouver Island, British Columbia, Canada

Visit Time: At least a two-day trip—possibly three!

☙❧

[*Breaking Dawn* Part 2 screenshot (enhanced)]

😠 Film-Site-Wise, Vancouver Island Earns a Skip-It Rating

- The *New Moon* and *Breaking Dawn* scenes shot here could have been filmed on almost any coastal beach in British Columbia—almost any coastal beach in the US states of Oregon or Washington—beaches far less time-consuming to visit.

- To reach the best (most distant) Vancouver Island film site beach is approximately **6 hours** via either ferry terminal on Vancouver Island to Nanaimo, not including the travel time from your Vancouver lodgings to the terminal. The 6 hour estimate includes arriving 45 minutes before the ferry's scheduled departure to assure your reservation, sailing time of approximately 2 hours, and drive time from the ferry to the farthest beach.

  It does not include visiting time on the island.

  Thus, even if you'll only be trekking to the film site beaches, truly enjoying a Twilight Saga Vancouver Island trip requires at least two days, with one overnight stay on the island.

As we so often discovered when researching other Vancouver area Twilight Saga film sites, however, there are tons of terrific non-*Twilight* attractions and activities available here. That is why we have awarded Vancouver Island a **Might-Be-Fun** rating, and will assist you to fully investigate this location before deciding whether or not you want to visit it.

ᘓᘔ

[Google Maps segments married & enhanced, ©2015 Google]

Vancouver Island

http://vancouverisland.com/
http://en.wikipedia.org/wiki/Vancouver_Island

Located in the southwestern corner of British Columbia, **Vancouver Island** is the largest island on the West Coast of North America. It was originally called **Quadra and Vancouver Island**, after the two 18th century explorers who "discovered" it: Spanish navigator Juan de la Bodega y Quadra, and British navy officer George Vancouver. Of course, Coast Salish First Nations peoples and other indigenous tribes had been living on the island for thousands of years before Quadra and Vancouver arrived.

From the Vancouver Island website:

> "Prepare yourself for the adventure of a lifetime on Vancouver Island, British Columbia, Canada. Explore Victoria, Tofino, Parksville, Campbell River or Port Hardy, or go hiking, camping, kayaking, golfing, salmon fishing, whale watching or wildlife viewing. Ranked ninth in Travel + Leisure magazine's 2014 World's Best Awards: Top Islands, Vancouver Island boasts magnificent rainforests, beaches, mountains, lakes and pristine rivers."

If you don't go whale-watching when visiting Steveston (**Site #34**), consider doing so here.

http://vancouverisland.com/things-to-do-and-see/whale-watching/
http://www.tourismvictoria.com/things-to-do/whale-watching/

Below are a couple other websites to explore when deciding whether or not Vancouver Island appeals to you.

http://www.hellobc.com/vancouver-island.aspx
http://www.vancouverisland.travel/

⊰⊱

[©2014 Blake Handley segment (enhanced)]

Victoria, British Columbia

http://www.tourismvictoria.com/
http://www.hellobc.com/victoria.aspx
http://en.wikipedia.org/wiki/Victoria,_British_Columbia

Although Vancouver is its largest city, the capital city of British Columbia is **Victoria**, which is located on Vancouver Island. Named after Queen Victoria, ruler of the United Kingdom when it first was settled by non-indigenous peoples in 1843, Victoria is one of the oldest cities in the Pacific Northwest.

On the Tourism Victoria website (link above) you'll find loads of information about the city, as well as a seasonal list of the many annual events and festivals that can be enjoyed during your visit. Victoria events and festivals represent an impressive diversity of cultures, as evidenced by the **Victoria Highland Games and Celtic Festival** in May, and the **Rifflandia Music Festival** in September.

http://victoriahighlandgames.com/
http://rifflandia.com/

Historic Architecture in Victoria

If historic architecture appeals to you, Victoria is an extremely attractive destination. Having painstakingly preserved many of its original buildings, as well as several structures erected just before WWI, the city is filled with fabulous examples of Victorian and Edwardian architecture.

http://www.hellobc.com/victoria/things-to-do/arts-culture-history/historic-heritage-sites.aspx
http://www.victoriaheritagefoundation.ca/
http://www.victoria.ca/EN/main/departments/planning-development/community-planning/heritage.html

Victoria also has a Hop-On/Hop-Off Big Bus

Whether driving or using public transportation to reach Vancouver Island, you may enjoy riding the Victoria Big Bus while visiting the city. Convenient and scenic, these guided tours can be fun.

http://bigbusvictoria.com

And Then, There are the Gardens!

"Victoria has long been known as the 'City of Gardens.' With our mild climate, gardening is a year-round passion which has resulted in an abundant array of gardens world renowned for their beauty and individual charm. That's why the International Garden Tourism Network awarded Victoria with the *International Garden Destination of the Year* award in 2015."

http://www.tourismvictoria.com/things-to-do/gardens-parks/

[©2012 Kathy Duval, Butchart Gardens]

Twilighters who enjoy spectacularly gorgeous gardens—viewed during a casual stroll *or* a serious hike—will be thrilled by a Victoria visit. Plan your own garden tour, or book one that is guided.
http://www.victoriafinest.bc.ca/guide-to-victoria/victoria-gardens-and-vancouver-island-parks
http://victoriangardentours.com/
http://www.heritagegardentours.ca/
http://vancouvertours.com/tour/victoria-tour/

Some of the Victoria whale-watching tour companies offer packages that include a Victoria garden visit.
http://princeofwhales.com/victoria-departures/whales-and-butchart-gardens-tour/
http://www.cvstours.com/whales-and-gardens.html
https://orcaspirit.com/packages/

And, at least two companies offer a **Vancouver** departure/return point for Victoria whale-watching excursions and garden tours—something that will save you from having to plan transportation between Vancouver and Vancouver Island independently.
http://www.clippervacations.com/multi-activity/whale-watching-butchart-gardens-day-trip-from-vancouver/
http://vancouvertours.com/tour/victoria-whales/

The Vancouver Island Dilemma

Being an *island*, getting to Vancouver Island isn't particularly quick or inexpensive.

> "There are no bridges connecting the island to the mainland, although the idea of building one has been brought up many times. ... The only vehicle access to Vancouver Island is via ferries operated by BC Ferries, Washington State Ferries and Black Ball Transport Inc."
>
> http://en.wikipedia.org/wiki/Vancouver_Island#Transport

Whether driving a rental car or riding on a public bus, a ferry boat is required to reach the island. The information below is based on fares available in April of 2015.

🚗 Victoria, Vancouver Island via Car:

- The one-way drive time from downtown Vancouver to Victoria—including the ferry ride—may take up to 4 hours.
- A one-way Ferry ride from the Tsawwassen Terminal (south of Vancouver) to the Swartz Bay Terminal (just northeast of Victoria) costs $17 per adult, plus $56 for the car.
- In total, a Vancouver/Victoria round-trip drive will cost $180 for 2 adults and one car ($90 each, if the expense is equally split), and require 8 hours of travel.

🚌 Victoria, Vancouver Island via Public Bus:

- The one-way bus travel time from downtown Vancouver to Victoria—including the ferry ride—is basically the same as driving there; up to 4 hours.
- The one-way Vancouver to Victoria bus fare costs $45 per adult, plus $17 each for the ferry ride.
- In total, the Vancouver/Victoria round-trip public bus ride will cost each adult $120, and require 8 hours of travel.

Because 8 hours are required for a Vancouver/Vancouver Island round-trip journey, it is possible to visit Victoria in one day. To visit the Twilight Saga beaches (even *without* going to Victoria), however, at least two days must be devoted to the trip—which means booking an overnight stay on the island.

To fully enjoy *both* Victoria and the Twilight Saga beaches, plan a three-day (two night) Vancouver Island visit.

[New Moon screenshot (enhanced)]

The Vancouver Island Film Sites

The "Quileute Reservation" beach scenes seen in *New Moon*, and both parts of *Breaking Dawn*, were shot at two—possibly three—beaches found on the southwestern coast of Vancouver Island. Happily, all of these beaches are within a few minutes of each other.

[Bing map segment (enhanced), ©2015 Nokia/Microsoft Corp]
http://www.TourTheTwilightSaga.com/B2/VBCtsMaps.pdf

We've included our Vancouver Island Twilight Saga Beaches map in the **Vancouver, BC Twilight Saga Maps PDF** freely posted on our website.

The beaches identified on our map are part of what Parks Canada calls the **Long Beach Unit**: 15 miles of beaches stretching between the Vancouver Island communities of **Tofino** and **Ucluelet**.
http://www.pc.gc.ca/eng/pn-np/bc/pacificrim/activ/activ12.aspx
http://www.tofino-bc.com/
http://en.wikipedia.org/wiki/Tofino
http://ucluelet.ca/
http://en.wikipedia.org/wiki/Ucluelet.

The Pacific Rim National Park Reserve

The Long Beach Unit is located within the Pacific Rim National Park Reserve.
http://www.pc.gc.ca/eng/pn-np/bc/pacificrim/index.aspx
http://en.wikipedia.org/wiki/Pacific_Rim_National_Park_Reserve

To visit these beaches you must purchase a **Park Use Permit** and display it in your vehicle. Park Use Permit revenue funds beach preservation, as well as visitor services and facility maintenance. The Park Use Permit you purchase allows you access to all of the Long Beach Unit beaches, car parks, hiking trails, and washrooms.
http://www.pc.gc.ca/pn-np/bc/pacificrim/visit/tarifs_fees_e.asp?park=21

Single-day Park Use Permits are available at kiosks found in each of the Twilight Saga film site beach car parks. Simply buy your permit at the first beach you visit.

2015 Fees: Adult $8, Senior $7, Youth $4. Group permits are also available.

Safety First!

When visiting any national park, you are responsible for ensuring your own safety, as well as for preserving the cultural and ecological integrity of the park. If you'll be visiting the Vancouver Island film site beaches, the website below is particularly helpful.
http://www.pc.gc.ca/eng/pn-np/bc/pacificrim/visit/visit7/visit7c.aspx

Please Read the Wildlife Warnings Appendix at the Back of this Book!

The Pacific Rim National Park Reserve is home to wild (freely-roaming), forest-dwelling animals such as bears, cougars, and *wolves* — as well as wild, shore-dwelling marine mammals such as seals and sea lions. It is your responsibility to know how to avoid attracting these potentially dangerous animals, as well as how to avoid conflict and protect yourself should an unexpected encounter occur.

When visiting British Columbia beaches, for instance, it is unlawful as well as dangerous to approach a marine mammal any closer than 100 meters (330 feet) — even if the animal is *dead*.

Sea lions in particular are known to carry a potentially lethal bacterial disease called **leptospirosis**, which can be transferred to humans. Never touch a dead marine mammal.

http://en.wikipedia.org/wiki/Leptospirosis
http://www.cdc.gov/leptospirosis/

> "In humans, [Leptospirosis] can cause a wide range of symptoms, some of which may be mistaken for other diseases. Some infected persons, however, may have no symptoms at all. Without treatment, Leptospirosis can lead to kidney damage, meningitis (inflammation of the membrane around the brain and spinal cord), liver failure, respiratory distress, and even death."

Beach Etiquette

Minimizing the impact of your visit is vitally important to the well-being of the many creatures that live on British Columbia beaches.

http://www.pc.gc.ca/eng/pn-np/bc/pacificrim/natcul/natcul2.aspx

"With 600,000 people visiting this park each year, human impact in the intertidal zone is significant. ... Remember the plants and animals on the rocks are alive, but dormant, awaiting the return of the tide and ocean water. Respect them as living things."

- **Avoid Scrunching, Grinding, and Stomping:** Look carefully when placing your feet—the surfaces you are walking on are covered with life. If you accidentally overturn a rock, be sure to protect the inhabitants that sought refuge beneath it by putting it back.
- **Avoid Prodding, Poking and Prying:** Explore gently. Never dislodge a marine creature from its rock or boulder.
- **Avoid Succumbing to the Full-Pockets- (Bags and Buckets) Syndrome!:** Leave the beach with memories and photographs—*only*. Not only is this an ecologically important guideline, it is illegal to remove artifacts such as shells, stones, driftwood, or seastars from British Columbia beaches.

The link below leads to a marvelous Parks Canada brochure, *Exploring the Seashore*. In addition to providing important safety tips and beach etiquette pointers, it contains descriptions that will help you identify the many forms of marine life you'll encounter. We highly recommend printing and bringing this brochure with you.

http://www.pc.gc.ca/~/media/pn-np/bc/pacificrim/pdf/rivage-shore_e.ashx

Tide Times

The best time to trek on any beach is at low tide. Low and high tide times change slightly with every succeeding day, based on changes in the sun and moon's position in relation to the beach's location on the earth.

Long Beach Unit low tide times occur twice a day, approximately 12 hours apart. In the Spring and mid-Summer months, low tide occurs very early in the morning and around 5-7pm. In August and the Fall, low tide occurs at mid-morning and early evening (8-10pm).

Visit the tide guide link below during your Twilight Saga trip preparation. Click on **Local Tide Reports Tofino & Ucluelet Tide Tables** to obtain tidal time predictions for the day of your visit.

http://www.naturalelementsrentals.com/tofino-ucluelet-tide-guide-area-23-and-24-tides-pacific-rim

Pack Out What You Pack In!

Rubbish bins are few and far between on the Long Beach Unit. Bring a small trash bag on your trek—tie it to the belt loop of your trousers or shorts, or stuff it in your backpack—and take your garbage with you when you leave.

To learn about Long Beach Unit dog policies and camping information, visit the website below.
http://www.pc.gc.ca/eng/pn-np/bc/pacificrim/visit/visit4c.aspx

None of the These Beaches Have Surf Guards on Duty

If you'll be dipping your toes—or actually engaging in water sports—be sure to read the Water Hazards webpage on the Parks Canada Pacific Rim National Park Reserve website while planning your trip.
http://www.pc.gc.ca/eng/pn-np/bc/pacificrim/visit/visit7/visit7g.aspx

ದ್ಞಲ

Finding the Vancouver Island Film Sites

Since the vast majority of Twilighters who trek here will be driving to the film site beaches from Vancouver Island ferry terminals, our directions begin with South Beach. Twihards who fly to Tofino and drive to the beaches from there can reverse the order of directions found below.

[New Moon screenshot (enhanced)]

South Beach

Nearest Car Park Google SatNav/GPS Coordinates: 49.013439, -125.673250

Drive Time from the Victoria Ferry Terminal: 4.5 hrs.

Drive Time from Nanaimo Terminals: 2 hrs, 45 min.

One of the two confirmed Vancouver Island Twilight Saga film sites, South Beach is a small, secluded beach, nestled at the base of a rocky promontory

that separates Wickaninnish Beach from Florencia Bay, where the *New Moon* scenes were shot of Jacob reviving Bella after her disastrous cliff jump.
http://www.vancouverislandaccommodations.com/parks/pacific-rim/south_beach/index.htm

> "South Beach is a sandy beach destination located in the Pacific Rim National Park ... The popular beach is both a hiking and beachcombing destination accessed via two different types of hiking trails. ...
>
> The short access route leading to the beach is only 1 kilometer long. It is easy, mostly flat and follows a boardwalk path through a rainforest to the beach. Just before the beach is a set of [short and not overly steep] stairs. ...
>
> Some of the summer activities enjoyed at South Beach include building sand castles, swimming, beachcombing, Frisbee, bocce ball, picnicking and hiking.
>
> Dressed in rain gear and rubber boots, people hike to South Beach in the winter months with binoculars for storm watching. Every year people come to watch the powerful storms crash the coastline, throwing logs and debris in the air.
>
> All visitors to the park must have a Park Use Permit. Pack out what you pack in."

According to the Parks Canada website:

> "South Beach offers spectacular, but potentially dangerous, wave watching. Very large waves and strong currents form at this pebble beach. Water activities not recommended."
>
> http://www.pc.gc.ca/eng/pn-np/bc/pacificrim/activ/activ12.aspx

[Google Street View image segment (enhanced), ©2014 Google]

On the west side of the nearest car park is a kiosk with a machine where you can purchase your Park Use Permit. The path next to it leads to the South Beach trailhead, as well as to …

[©2013 frtzw906]

The Kwisitis Visitor Centre

http://www.pc.gc.ca/eng/pn-np/bc/pacificrim/activ/activkwisitis.aspx
http://tofinohiatus.com/tofinohikes/nuu-chah-nulth-trail/kwisitis-visitor-centre.html

"The Kwisitis Visitor Centre is a beautiful and astonishingly elaborate little museum next to the very nice Kwisitis Feast House (previously the Wickaninnish Restaurant). Both the Centre and the Restaurant lay in the rainforest of Quisitis Point that separates Wickaninnish Beach and Florencia Bay. …

The Kwisitis Visitor Centre exhibits are stunning. A full size recreation of a whale hunt takes up much of the main room. The attention to detail is amazing as you can see the intensity in the hunter's faces as they go for the kill. Several other depictions line the walls."

http://www.venturevancouver.com/kwisitis-visitor-centre-pacific-rim-national-park

"The Kwisitis Visitors Centre also overlooks Wickaninnish beach. Eagle eyed visitors can often spot a variety of animals from the viewing deck outside or on the second story of the Centre— including whales, seals, sea lions and bears, and during low tide, explore the rock pools which form on the rocky outcrops on the beach below."

Open daily between March and September from 10am to 4:30pm (until 5:30pm in summer months), admission to the Kwisitis Visitor Centre is included in your Park Use Permit fee. If you'll be trekking to South Beach, we strongly suggest setting aside at least two hours to tour this marvelous museum and catch a bite to eat at the **Kwisitis Feast House**.
http://www.kwisitisfeasthouse.com/

The South Beach Trail

Follow signs from the car park or the Kwisitis Visitors Centre to find the rain forest trail that leads to South Beach, and follow it.

After a short distance, you'll pass a picnic area.

Soon after passing the picnic area you may notice paths on your right that lead to a tiny beach. That isn't South Beach. Stay on the trail.

Next, you'll arrive at the **Nuu-Chah-Nulth Trailhead** intersection.
http://tofinohiatus.com/tofinohikes/nuu-chah-nulth-trail.html

This trail leads to the Florencia Bay beach. It is a 2.5 km (1.5 mile) hike with lots of up-and-down sections. Continue on the South Beach trail—there's an easier way to reach Florencia Bay, and we'll tell you about it below.

When you reach several short sets of wooden stairs, you'll be approaching South Beach.

Please Note: According to satellite map images, it appears possible to walk from the south end of Wickaninnish Beach to the tiny beach, and join the South Beach trail there. We suspect that this access is only available during low tide. Thus, we do not recommend using this route. Tides can change quickly.

[New Moon screenshot (enhanced)]

The moment you set foot on South Beach you'll recognize where the screenshot above was shot. Enjoy!

While wandering here, keep your eyes open for background landmarks seen in the mystery film site screenshots below. *Breaking Dawn* Part 1 Wolf Pack beach scenes *may* have been shot on South Beach.

[Breaking Dawn Part 1 screenshot (enhanced)]

The Mystery Film Site Beach

In *Breaking Dawn* Part 1, while Bella and Edward were honeymooning on **Isle Esme** (TTTS Book Four: Film Sites in Other USA States—and Around the World), the movie cut to scenes of Quileute Wolf Pack members enjoying some beach time; presumably on First Beach at La Push. Imprinted members were seen playing soccer and picnicking with their mates, while Jacob and un-imprinted individuals looked on, discussing the pros and cons of imprinting.

The Wolf Pack chapter of *BDP1* DVD Special Features contains behind-the-scene footage of the beach where these scenes were shot in 2011. Below are comments made by director Bill Condon within that chapter:

> "We shot at the same beach at Tofino that the other movies had shot at, and got really lucky. It was a tough scene to do in a short time, but I remember that as being one of our more blessed days."

Condon's comments seem to be a very straight forward indication of these *BDP1* scenes having been shot at the northern end of Long Beach (near Tofino), where many of the *New Moon* beach scenes were filmed—a beach film site confirmed by respected Internet sources such as the **Internet Movie Data Base** (IMDb).

http://www.imdb.com/title/tt1259571/locations?ref_=tt_dt_dt

However! The IMDb and other Internet sources credit **Ucluelet, British Columbia** as being the film site for *BDP1* Wolf Pack beach scenes.
http://www.imdb.com/title/tt1324999/locations?ref_=tt_dt_dt
http://en.wikipedia.org/wiki/The_Twilight_Saga:_Breaking_Dawn_%E2%80%93_Part_1

We searched for a "Ucluelet Beach" on Vancouver Island and discovered that there isn't one. So, we continued searching. The best *BDP1* Wolf Pack beach film site location clue we could find was a *Westerly News* article published in March of 2011.
http://www.westerlynews.ca/local-news/twilight-film-crew-returns-to-west-coast-1.187303

> "A convoy of trailers and buses is stationed at the Wya Welcome Centre parking lot at the Tofino-Ucluelet junction, indicating the presence of a movie crew for the shooting of scenes for the popular Twilight vampire series. Toni Atterbury, publicist for the movie, was able to confirm that filming for the fourth and fifth movies in the series is taking place. ... Atterbury was mum on answering further questions in terms of how long crews would be filming in the area or where the actual filming is taking place."

The Wya Welcome Centre is directly across the highway from the **Pacific Rim Visitor Centre**. Both are located at the junction of the Pacific Rim Highway (Hwy 4) and the Tofino-Ucluelet Highway.
http://www.ucluth.ca/wya-welcome-centre-ucluelet
http://www.pacificrimvisitor.ca

Google SatNav/GPS: 2791 Pacific Rim Hwy, Ucluelet, BC V0R 3A0
[**BTW:** We highly recommend visiting both of these facilities.]

Considering the fact that there are plenty of potential support vehicle staging locations far closer to the confirmed *New Moon* film site at Long Beach's Tofino end—16 km/10 miles north of the Tofino-Ucluelet junction—we suspect that 2011 Wolf Pack beach scenes may have been shot on South Beach ... or on Wickaninnish Beach.

After all, although South Beach isn't credited by IMDb (or other Internet sources) as a *New Moon* film site, it is a confirmed *New Moon* Vancouver Island beach film site.

Additionally, because both South Beach and Wickaninnish Beach are at the southern end of the Long Beach Unit, they are nearer to Ucluelet than to Tofino—which would explain the Ucluelet film site credit.

Then, Again, We Could Be Dead Wrong!

It is entirely possible that filmmakers used a more distant support vehicle staging site in hopes of keeping the curious from making their way to the Tofino end of Long Beach during 2011 beach filming.

But, that still doesn't explain the Ucluelet film site credit.

This is why we suggest that you eyeball the *Breaking Dawn* Part 1 screen-shots below while wandering on South Beach. If you don't recognize the background landmarks there, consider visiting Wickaninnish Beach next.

Wickaninnish Beach

During our initial research, we decided that the best candidate for the mystery *BDP*1 Wolf Pack beach film site was the southern end of Wickaninnish Beach. Happily, this beach can be reached from the same path that leads west from the South Beach/Kwisitis Visitors Centre car park.

In fact, the first place you'll reach when following this path is a simple, yet moving, memorial to Canadian Foreign War Veterans. To the right of the memorial is a short path to Wickaninnish Beach.

[©2015 carlykb.com]

Memorial plaques commemorating Canadian Foreign War Veterans have been erected in at least one national park within each of Canada's ten provinces. The inscription on these memorial plaques reads:

> "They will never know the beauty of this place, see the seasons change, enjoy nature's chorus. All we enjoy we owe to them, men and women who lie buried in the earth of foreign lands and in the seven seas. Dedicated to the memory of Canadians who died overseas in the service of their country and so preserved our heritage."

http://www.veterans.gc.ca/eng/news/viewrelease/1178

Upon reaching Wickaninnish Beach from this path, turn left and head to the section of beach found south of the overlooking Kwisitis Visitors Centre.

[Google "Street View" image segment (enhanced), ©2014 Greg Sutherland]

Thanks to non-street location photography available via Google Maps' Street View function, we were able to virtually visit Wickaninnish Beach. The image above is of the southern-most end. Lo and behold, it looks very much like the background seen in the *BD*P1 screenshot below.

[Breaking Dawn Part 1 screenshot (enhanced)]

[Breaking Dawn Part 1 Special Features screenshot segment (enhanced)]

In the *BDP*1 DVD Special Features Wolf Pack chapter, this film site beach's northern end is also seen. Unfortunately, the northern end of the southern Wickaninnish Beach section (below) looks nothing like the screenshot above.

[Google "Street View" image segment (enhanced), ©2014 Greg Sutherland]

That's the Kwisitis Visitors Centre in the distance—something not seen in any portion of the *BDP*1 Wolf Pack Special Features. Thus, we have decided that Wickaninnish Beach probably isn't the Wolf Pack beach film site.

Florencia Bay Beach

Wick Road Turn Google SatNav/GPS Coordinates: 49.013777, -125.651396

Nearest Car Park Google SatNav/GPS Coordinates: 49.013439, -125.673250

http://tofinohiatus.com/tofinohikes/florencia-bay.html
http://www.tofinotime.com/beaches/florenciabay.htm

We didn't see any Wolf Pack beach screenshot landmarks when looking at the few Florencia Bay images available. Thus, we do not believe that *BDP*1 filming took place on Florencia Bay's beach.

If you wish to visit this beach and see for yourself, however, return to the South Beach/Kwisitis Visitors Centre car park and drive back to Wick Road. Turn right and drive east for approximately 2 minutes, until you see a sign indicating the right turn to **Florencia Bay Beach Access**.

After driving about 2 minutes south on that road you'll arrive at the Florencia Bay Beach Access car park. Park and hike to the beach.

Long Beach and Incinerator Rock

http://tofinohiatus.com/tofinohikes/long-beach.html

"Long Beach is the wonderfully accessible beach that spans the middle of Pacific Rim National Park for several kilometers. It's the longest stretch of surf swept sand on the west coast of Vancouver

Island. In fact, if you include Florencia Bay, Wickaninnish Beach, Combers Beach and Schooner Cove with Long Beach, then it is the longest sand dune on Vancouver Island."

The Long Beach *New Moon* film sites are found at Incinerator Rock, which juts up from the northern end of Long Beach, immediately south of the Tofino Airport.

[New Moon screenshot (enhanced)]
http://twifans.com/profiles/blogs/new-moon-set-pictures
http://www.movie-locations.com/movies/t/Twilight_New_Moon.html#.UUDDXDdhuSo

"After being outed as a werewolf, Jacob walks with Bella on the beach at Incinerator Rock at Long Beach, where he explains to her that lycanthropy is not a lifestyle choice, he was born that way."

[©2013 Samantha Challand]

Within minutes of reaching Long Beach from the northern end of Incinerator Rock's car park, you'll recognize the *New Moon* screenshot location above.

[New Moon screenshot (enhanced)]

The film site where the Jacob/Bella conversation continued should be found on Long Beach, just south of Incinerator Rock.

Unfortunately, while perusing virtual images of Long Beach—both north and south of Incinerator Rock—we couldn't find any of the background landmarks seen in the mystery *BDP1* Wolf Pack beach screenshots.

If you journey to Vancouver Island Twilight Saga beaches and discover the actual Wolf Pack beach film site, please Email CD Miller to report your findings: chas@novelholiday.com

The Long Beach and Incinerator Rock Car Parks

Incinerator Rock Car Park Google SatNav/GPS Coordinates: 49.072812, -125.764939

Long Beach Car Park Google SatNav/GPS Coordinates: 49.071336,-125.757322

According to the Tofino BC website, the Incinerator Rock car park is so small that it often is full.
http://tofino-bc.com/blog/tofino-beaches/long-beach/

> "The more northerly parking lot, at the Incinerator Rock sign, is usually full in the summer months, as it has the quickest access to the surf. This parking lot can be hectic with surfers stopping by to check the surf. If you have your heart set on parking here, arrive early and stake your claim. Be prepared for the occasional bare bum as many harmless surfers change here into their wetsuits.

The larger Long Beach parking area is just down the highway another 500 metres south. Turn at the Long Beach sign. Here you can almost always find vacant parking spaces and the short trails leading down to the beach are easy to walk and wheelchair accessible. If you are going to the beach to picnic, it is generally not worth fighting for a parking spot at Incinerator Rock. This Long Beach parking area is a lovely spot in itself and the landscaped areas adjacent to the pavement can provide a nice respite from the summer sun. Fewer surfers come here to park, preferring the more immediate beach access at Incinerator Rock."

When heading here from the South Beach/Kwisitis Visitors Centre car park—approximately a 15 minute drive—you'll see the Long Beach sign first. Another minute north of that is the Incinerator Rock sign. Considering how close they are, there's no harm in checking the Incinerator Rock car park first.

Both of these parking lots have Park Use Permit kiosks and public toilets.

Please Note: When planning your Vancouver Island Twilight Saga film site beaches visit, the most important location to reach during low tide is Incinerator Rock at Long Beach. Thus, we're reprising the tide guide link offered earlier.

http://www.naturalelementsrentals.com/tofino-ucluelet-tide-guide-area-23-and-24-tides-pacific-rim

If you'll be visiting Vancouver Island beaches in late Summer or Fall, consider heading to Incinerator Rock first—when the morning low tide time is around 8-10am.

Unless you are an inveterate early-riser, schedule your Spring or early Summer Vancouver Island beaches trek backwards from the late afternoon/ early evening low tide time at Incinerator Rock. Unfortunately, this method of scheduling will require you to set estimated time limits at South Beach, the Kwisitis Visitors Centre, and Wickaninnish Beach. Be generous! After coming this far, it is better to find yourself waiting a while before being able to fully enjoy the Incinerator Rock film site, than to have to cut your visits short elsewhere.

Going to Vancouver Island

Begin by deciding what you want to visit on Vancouver Island: Victoria, the Twilight Saga beaches, or both. Next, decide on the time you're willing to take for the trip.

- One day to visit Victoria, only.
  (The Twilight Saga beaches cannot be visited in one day.)
- Two days (one night) to visit the Twilight Saga beaches, and possibly squeeze in a trip to Victoria.
- Three days (two nights) to fully enjoy *both* Victoria and the Twilight Saga beaches.

After those decisions, all that remains is planning how you'll get there.

🚌 Via Public Transportation

The Trip Advisor article below is a marvelous public transport information resource:
http://www.tripadvisor.com/Travel-g154943-c5611/Vancouver:British-Columbia:Getting.From.Vancouver.To.Victoria.html

The Tourism Vancouver "Victoria—Getting There" webpage is also very helpful:
http://www.tourismvancouver.com/go/day-trips/victoria/getting-there/

As are the several Vancouver Island Travel website "Getting Here" pages:
http://www.vancouverisland.travel/

✈ By Air

Twihards can fly to Victoria International Airport (YYJ), Nanaimo Airport (YCD), or Tofino-Long Beach Airport (YAZ) from Vancouver. You can even fly to Vancouver Island airports from **Seattle** or **Port Angeles**. (TTTS Book One—the Olympic Peninsula.) If interested in flying to Vancouver Island, explore the websites below.
http://mytofino.com/travel-methods/tofino-flights/
http://www.tourismtofino.com/getting-to-tofino/air
http://www.tofinoairport.com/
http://www.vancouverisland.travel/transportation/air-service/
http://www.tourismvictoria.com/plan/getting-here/airlines-floatplanes/

Please Note: Rental cars are available at any Vancouver Island airport. When flying to the smaller airports (Nanaimo or Tofino), however, be sure to book your car well in advance. Otherwise, you may find yourself marooned at the airport.

🚗 Driving to Vancouver Island from Vancouver

Start by identifying the mainland ferry terminal closest to your Vancouver area lodgings.

Vancouver Tsawwassen Terminal
#1 Ferry Causeway, Delta, BC V4M 4G6; 49.024813, -123.105031

This is the closest terminal if you lodge near Vancouver International Airport, or in points south and east of the city.

West Vancouver, Horseshoe Bay Terminal
6750 Keith Road, West Vancouver, BC V7W 2V1
49.374208, -123.272176

This is the closest terminal if you lodge in West Vancouver, or in points north and east of that area.

Explore the BC Ferries Website and Explore Ferry Schedules
http://www.bcferries.com/schedules/mainland/

Visiting the Twilight Saga Film Site Beaches Only
Travel to and from one of the two Nanaimo, Vancouver Island ferry terminals.

Nanaimo, Duke Point Terminal
(Ferries from the Tsawwassen Terminal)
400 Duke Point Hwy, Nanaimo, BC V9X 1H6
49.161730, -123.891861

Nanaimo, Departure Bay Terminal
(Ferries from the Horseshoe Bay Terminal)
680 Trans Canada Highway, Nanaimo, BC V9S 5R1
49.178832, -123.945002

Please Note: Although the Tsawwassen Terminal offers ferries to Nanaimo and may be closer to your Vancouver lodgings, it might be faster to use the Horseshoe Bay Terminal as your departure/return terminal.

Visiting Victoria Only
Ferries to Victoria aren't available from Horseshoe Bay Terminal. Thus, no matter where you lodge in the Vancouver area, you'll need to book both of your one-way (outbound and return) ferry tickets between the Vancouver Tsawwassen Terminal and Victoria's Swartz Bay Terminal.

Victoria Swartz Bay Terminal
North Saanich, BC V8L 5J4
48.688718, -123.410954

Visiting the Twilight Saga Film Site Beaches *and* Victoria
Based on where you're lodging and what you'll be visiting **first** (Victoria or the beaches), it may be best to arrive at the Victoria Swartz Bay terminal and leave from one of the Nanaimo terminals—or vice versa. Additionally, it may save time to use two different mainland terminals for your departure

and return points. Since all Vancouver/Vancouver Island ferry tickets are one-way, this is easily accomplished.

After finding ferry schedules that work best for you, book both of them. Each ferry terminal sells unreserved one-way tickets. Individuals without a reservation, however, are considered **stand-by travelers.** If a ferry is fully-booked (as they often are in summer months), you may have to wait for the next one—possibly even the one after that. That is why it is important to book tickets in advance.

Once your ferry reservations are secured, be sure to plan your outbound and return terminal arrival times at least 45 to 60 minutes before the scheduled sailing time. According to BC Ferries:

> "Reservations should be claimed at the ticket booth 45 to 60 minutes prior to the scheduled sailing time. If you are not checked in 30 minutes prior to the scheduled sailing time your reservation will no longer be valid and you will travel stand-by. ... The reservation fee for unclaimed [invalidated] reservations will not be refunded."

Plot Your Driving Journey

There is prominent signage on all Vancouver and Vancouver Island highway approaches to ferry terminals. Twilighters with a SatNav/GPS device, however, will appreciate the addresses and coordinates provided above for plotting the journey from your Vancouver area lodgings to the mainland terminal, and your journey back to the island terminal from the beaches.

Coordinates for the Twilight Saga Beaches Car Parks

South Beach and the Southern End of Wickaninnish Beach
Nearest Car Park: 49.013439, -125.673250

Florencia Bay Beach
Wick Road Turn: 49.013777, -125.651396
Nearest Car Park: 49.013439, -125.673250

Long Beach and Incinerator Rock Car Parks
Incinerator Rock Car Park: 49.072812, -125.764939
Long Beach Car Park: 49.071336,-125.757322

Victoria Visit Destination Addresses and Coordinates

Because we cannot possibly anticipate what sites you'll want to see when visiting the fabulous city of Victoria, you'll need to research the addresses/coordinates for them on your own.

Twilighters who can afford a two- or three-day trip to Vancouver Island will *not* be disappointed!

Inaccessible

Inaccessible Vancouver, BC, Twilight Saga Film Sites

A few of the known Vancouver, BC, Twilight Saga film sites are entirely inaccessible because they're located on private property or within private residences. And, sadly, one Vancouver film site that was publicly accessible prior to 2013 has since been completely demolished.

To save you tons of time searching for these sites—thinking that we missed them—they are listed below.

[*Eclipse* Special Features screenshot (enhanced)]

Jasper's Flashback Barn

In August of 2009, on a rural property located within Langley Township (southeast of Vancouver, BC), an *Eclipse* night shoot took place inside a barn that is over 100 years old. The scenes filmed here were Jasper's flashbacks about training newborns for his maker, Maria, in the late 1800s.

[Internet-posted pic segment (enhanced), ©2009 natspov.blogspot.com]
http://natspov.blogspot.com/2009/08/twilight-saga-eclipse-set-exploring.html

This property is a family-owned business whose obligation to the Twilight movie franchise ended when *Eclipse* shooting wrapped at this location. When we contacted them in 2014, the family replied:

> "Thanks for your interest in exposing our farm as it relates to a very brief Twilight location shoot. We had a taste of [Twilight fan enthusiasm] after the shoot and again after the movie came out, and will decline taking part in any further visits from Twilighters. We ask that Twilighters respect our privacy and property."

[©2013 CD Miller]

Even if you could somehow gain entry to it, the old barn's interior looks nothing like what was seen on screen—it is packed full of modern farm machinery and the floor is completely free of hay. Thus, there are no screenshot reproduction photo opportunities here.

[Bing Maps bird's eye segment (enhanced), ©2015 Microsoft Corp]

Parthenon Park

Parthenon Park is a very private, beachfront park located in a well-to-do West Vancouver neighborhood. If you Google "Parthenon Park, Vancouver, BC" (or anything similar to that), the only references that will pop up are for home sales in the area. Because it is completely private, Parthenon Park isn't listed on any of the official Vancouver or British Columbia park websites.

A few Twilight Saga Internet resources cite Parthenon Park as a *New Moon* film site—which is sort of true. All that was shot here, however, were background plates of some cliffs that later were CGI-enhanced before being used to replace the green screens mounted behind studio footage filmed of wolf pack and Victoria stunt-doubles cliff-jumping.

[©2013 CD Miller]

Another Cullen House

While the address of this West Vancouver dwelling is posted all over the Internet as a *New Moon* film site, only interior Cullen House scenes were filmed at this private residence. Extremely brief *New Moon* Cullen House exterior footage was shot at the same location as for *Twilight*: the Hoke House in Portland, Oregon (TTTS Book Three).

[*New Moon* SF screenshot segment (enhanced)] [Internet-posted photo segment, ©unknown]
http://freshome.com/2009/11/21/twilight-new-moon-film-house-for-sale/#.UMd_N6zheSo

After *New Moon* filming wrapped, this delightfully contemporary dwelling was sold for over three million dollars. Since you cannot go inside the house, there are absolutely no screenshot reproduction photo opportunities available here.

[*Breaking Dawn* Part 2 Special Features screenshot segment (enhanced)]

The Cullen House *Breaking Dawn* Set Location

For *Eclipse*, almost all of the Cullen House was built on a sound stage—the exterior designed to look exactly like the Hoke House in Portland, the interior design based on the architectural aspects of rooms seen in *Twilight* and *New Moon*. For *Breaking Dawn*, however, filmmakers spent over one million dollars to build the entire Cullen House on a river-side patch of private property located in a remote area near Squamish, British Columbia.

[*Breaking Dawn* Part 1 screenshot segment (enhanced)]

For the first time we got to see the back of the Cullen House—something specially designed for the film. This film site also is where all the wedding scenes were shot.

[©2014 **Twilight Girl Portland** photo segment (enhanced)]

Because absolutely nothing of the house or wedding set remains to be seen, there is no point in searching for this property's location—no point in trespassing here should you find it. According to Twilight Girl Portland:

> "When we found the right driveway it had a locked chain across it with no trespassing signs. ... We figured out where the house was and where the wedding took place. After spending time there we were down by the river when I turned and noticed a woman far back with her dog. Uh Oh. ... We learned that the woman owns the property and lived down the driveway next to this one. She lives right there so I would not recommend going in. She said she couldn't believe that fans were still coming on her property. I guess she just doesn't understand the TWILIGHT FANDOM."
>
> http://twilightgirlportland.com/breaking-dawn-movie-location-cullen-house-squamish/

While we completely understand "TWILIGHT FANDOM," we do not recommend trespassing on this film site. It simply isn't worth the time and trouble.

[*New Moon* screenshot (enhanced)] [twilightsaga.wikia.com photo segment (enhanced)

The Ridge Theatre in Vancouver

All of the *New Moon* interior scenes of Jacob, Mike, and Bella's Port Angeles movie theatre trip to watch *Face Punch* were shot inside the iconic Ridge Theatre, which once was located at 3131 Arbutus Street in Vancouver. Alas and alack, although it had been in operation since 1950, the Ridge Theatre was closed down in February of 2013.
http://www.huffingtonpost.ca/2013/02/03/ridge-theatre-closed-vancouver_n_2612800.html?

[©2013 CD Miller]

In September of 2013, the Ridge Theatre and it's attached bowling alley were still there, but were fenced off and awaiting demolition. At that time, we still had hope that the various Friends of the Ridge Theatre groups would be successful in preventing the Ridge's demise.

[Google Maps Street View image segment (enhanced), ©2014 Google]

Unfortunately, in July of 2014, Google Maps Street View demonstrated that the Ridge is gone forever.

Appendices

Tips for Twilighting in Canada

Planning and preparation is important to enjoying the most Twilicious possible tour of British Columbia — or, anywhere *else*, for that matter.

To accommodate the needs of Twilighters around the world, we created **TwiTips** PDFs that address a variety of planning and preparation issues, and posted them online. Some Twilighters will wish to read all of them — others, only a few.

You can access the TwiTips PDF titles listed below, without charge, on the **TwiTips & Maps** directory page of *Tour the Twilight Saga* **Book Two**'s website.
http://tourthetwilightsaga.com/vancouver-british-columbia/book-two-twitips-maps/

⋆**Please Note:** Book Two's TwiTips & Maps directory page also contains links to:

Our Vancouver Twilight Saga Maps PDF

Rather than posting an individual map for each Twilight Saga site, we put *all* of our maps into one PDF. Print and pack the pages (maps) important to the places you'll be visiting.

A TwiLinks PDF for Each Chapter

TwiLinks are files containing all of the **website reference addresses** found within each Twilight Saga site chapter — as well as within the book's front matter and appendix. After opening any TwiLinks PDF on your desktop or laptop computer, you can simply *click on* each of the reference links, rather than having to type website addresses into your Internet browser.

Tour the Twilight Saga Book Two TwiTips PDFs

Vancouver, BC Twilight Saga Trip Planning Tips

Whether journeying to British Columbia from another Canadian province, the US or another foreign country, this PDF provides tips important to:

- Selecting the Twilight Saga Sites you want to visit.
- Deciding on the dates of your trip.
- Determining how long you'll need for your Twilight Saga holiday.
- Planning a Vancouver visit.
- Staying safe when Twilighting in British Columbia.
- Special British Columbia packing pointers.

Lodgings in and around Vancouver, BC

Tips for selecting and booking the place you'll stay while Twilighting in British Columbia.

Info for International Twilighters

Tips important to US and other foreign national Twilighters who will be traveling to Canada.

Telephones and Internet Access when Twilighting in British Columbia

- How to decide between using your own cell phone (mobile) while visiting Canada, or to rent/purchase one.
- The hidden dangers of using a smart phone while visiting a foreign country.
- Options for safely accessing the Internet when visiting a foreign country or another Canadian province.

Important Phone Number Info for Twication Planning and Traveling

- Calling between countries when planning your trip and while Twilighting.
- Emergency phone numbers in Canada.
- Operator assistance in Canada.
- Phone numbers for foreign national embassies in Canada.

Vancouver, BC Airport Options

Tips to assist Canadian, US and other foreign national Twilighters who plan to fly to Vancouver, Victoria, *or* Seattle, Washington.

Vancouver, BC Public Transportation Options

- Taking a train to Vancouver.
- Bussing to Vancouver.
- Public transportation from Vancouver International Airport to Downtown.
- Public transportation within and around Vancouver.

Our Rental Car TwiTips Collection

Car Rental TwiTips

- Basic tips for avoiding unnecessary rental charges.
- Suggestions for selecting a car that will best meet your needs.
- The value of bringing or renting a SatNav/GPS device.

Rental Car Checklist

Download this check list to your smart phone, or print and pack it. Follow the check list before leaving the car rental lot to avoid a plethora of problems (and additional expenses) while Twilighting.

The Right-Side Driving Dilemma

Twilighters who live in left-side driving countries (e.g., Australia, Japan, India, Malaysia, Singapore, the UK) may experience anxiety or confusion when driving on the right side of the road in the US or Canada. This PDF describes methods of diminishing right-side-driving anxiety and tips to help avoid accidents.

Automatic Transmission Anxieties

The vast majority of Canadian and US rental cars are equipped with an automatic transmission. Twilighters accustomed to operating a manual (standard) transmission vehicle will find these tips helpful.

Canadian Driving Details

Whether driving your personal vehicle to British Columbia, or renting a car after your arrival, this TwiTips PDF provides the following valuable information:

- Canadian license requirements.
- Driving regulations and parking practices in Canada.
- Important Canadian speed limits and gas (petrol) information.
- Tips for driving in the city of Vancouver.
- Paper maps vs Apps … and much, much more!

Speed Limit Conversion Tables

These tables are helpful for US Twilighters driving a US automobile (MPH speedometer) to Canada—as well as for Canadian Twilighters driving a Canadian automobile (KM/H speedometer) to the US.

Universal Twilighter Packing Pointers

Whether journeying to British Columbia from another Canadian province, the US or another foreign country, this PDF will help you decide what to pack and how to pack it.

Photography and Packing Pointers

- What kind of camera(s) to bring.
- How to pack your cameras and photography accessories (including batteries and memory cards).
- General photography tips for accomplishing the best possible Twication photo record.

Supplies to Purchase after You Arrive

No matter where in the world you're Twilighting, if something can be purchased cheaply *after* reaching your destination, you'll not need to pack it. The smaller, lighter, and fewer your bags are, the less you'll have to pay to bring them with you.

This PDF provides tips for quickly finding the most convenient Canadian discount store after your arrival (no matter how you get to Vancouver), and a basic shopping list of items to buy in Canada rather than pack.

British Columbia Wildlife Warnings

Be Prepared for Wild Animal Encounters—*Wherever* You Go in British Columbia

Wilderness areas in British Columbia are teeming with wild animals that are free to roam wherever they wish. Many of these animals can be dangerous if you get too close or encounter one accidentally while Twilighting.

[Photos published by Kenneth Chan, Vancity Buzz, ©2014]

Because so many BC cities and towns are adjacent to wilderness areas, a wild animal encounter is possible within highly populated places. The photo above left is of a black bear roaming the Simon Fraser University campus, approximately 8 miles (13 km) east of downtown Vancouver's **Gastown** area (Site #31). Above right is a photo of a coyote seen so often on the University of British Columbia campus that students have named him "Carter." UBC is only 7 miles (11 km) west of Gastown.

http://www.vancitybuzz.com/2014/11/resident-campus-animals-sfu-bear-ubc-coyote-sightings-photos-videos/

> "Bear sightings at the [SFU] campus are not uncommon, and in most cases where the animal becomes too comfortable with humans they are tranquilized and relocated. ..."

There are thousands of urban coyotes living in Metro Vancouver, including hundreds at UBC's Pacific Spirit Regional Park, and they are highly adaptable as long as they are able to find food and shelter.

However, these animals can potentially become dangerous to humans when they lose their timidness and instinctual fear of humans."

Especially when visiting a wilderness area, it is your responsibility to know how to avoid close encounters with wild animals, as well as how to protect yourself should an unexpected encounter occur.

[Eclipse Special Features screenshot segment (enhanced)]

Sites Where Wild Animal Encounters are Likely

- **Gilleys Trail, Coquitlam; Jacob Black's House** (Site #25)
  Bobcats and black bears are frequently seen in this area. In 2009, the black bear above surprised cast and crew during *Eclipse* filming at Jacob's house.
       Parts of Minnekhada Park (immediately east of Gilleys Trail) are commonly closed when bear activity is particularly high. Black bear encounters are also possible within nearby cities, such as Port Coquitlam.
  http://bc.ctvnews.ca/large-black-bear-forces-lockdown-at-port-coquitlam-school-1.2024759

- **Widgeon Slough Marsh, Coquitlam; Motorcycle Lessons** (Site #26)
  Only a few miles northeast of Minnekhada Park, the Widgeon Slough area also is frequented by black bears and bobcats.
- **Sasamat Lake, Belcarra Regional Park** (Site #28)
  Black bears found wandering on the SFU campus are often thought

to have swum across the narrow Burrard Inlet channel from Belcarra Regional Park on the north shore.

- **Pemberton, Home of the Denali Coven** (Site #35)
  Being a remote mountain location, both grizzly and black bears freely roam this area, as do cougars, lynx, bobcats, wolves, coyotes, foxes, and wolverines.
- **Vancouver Island** (Site #37)
  The beaches of Vancouver Island present a special wildlife encounter challenge. Not only do the island's forest-dwelling denizens (bears, cougars, and wolves) come to feed on beached fish, marine mammals such as seals and sea lions live here. If you come too near them, these seemingly innocent, cuddly-looking characters can be just as dangerous as bears, cougars, or wolves.

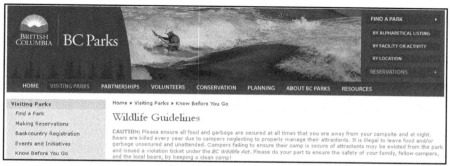

[©http://www.env.gov.bc.ca]

Know Before You Go

Please visit the **British Columbia Parks** website and review their general Wildlife Guidelines, as well as the bear, cougar, and wolf guideline links offered.
http://www.env.gov.bc.ca/bcparks/explore/wild_gen.html

The **British Columbia Conservation Foundation**'s **WildSafeBC** website is another marvelous reference, where you can learn about:

- Bears
- Deer
- Rattlesnakes

- Cougars
- Moose
- Skunks

- Coyotes
- Raccoons

(We have no idea why they left wolves out.)
https://wildsafebc.com/species/

Basic Rules for Wildlife Encounters

- **Make noise** when Twi-hiking in the wilderness—talking, laughing, singing—to alert wild animals of your approach and allow them to leave.
- **View from a distance.** Avoid coming closer than 100 yards/meters. (The length of an American football field.)
- **Never approach animals**, especially during the months of May through August when they may be protecting young.
- **Speak softly and BACK away.** If you unexpectedly come upon wildlife close up, avoid noises or actions that might stress animals or cause them to waste energy in unnecessary flight. Speaking softly and backing away will (hopefully) prevent you from triggering a chase response.
- If the animal doesn't leave, **yell, shout, blow a whistle.**
- **Do Not Feed Wildlife of any kind!** Feeding leads to problems such as habituation to humans ("a fed bear is a dead bear"), unnatural food dependency, disease or even death.

What follows are some quick reminders for what to do if you accidentally have a close-up wild animal encounter while Twilighting. It's a good idea to review all of these tips each time you're about to trek into a wilderness area. After all, you'll not have time to look them up when you suddenly stumble upon a cougar, or bear, or wolf.

If you have an animal encounter, call **the Conservation Officer Service** at **1-877-952-7277** to report:

- Animals that lack fear of humans or display aggression towards humans.
- Incidents of environmental violation (feeding wild animals, leaving food out).
- Poaching.

[©2015 http://revelstokebearaware.org/]

Bear Safety

- Do not turn and run!
- Pick up small children (or pets) so they cannot panic and flee.
- AVOID direct eye contact.
- Speak softly at first.
- BACK away slowly at first, then more rapidly.

If the bear doesn't leave the area, continue backing away and begin **shouting and waving your arms**. "Get-the-hell-outta-here, Bear! Shoo! Go away!" Blowing a whistle is also effective.

If the bear starts to follow you, it's probably because your travel bag smells tasty. **Abandon your bag** and continue backing away. As soon as the bear is preoccupied with your bag, turn and quickly leave the area.

Trees are *not* a means of escape. Bears are surprisingly agile in trees. They can climb far faster and higher than you can.

Playing dead does *not* work. If attacked, fight back!

Strike the bear with anything you can reach—sticks, stones, or your fists. Since the bulk of its body is well padded, aim for its face to cause discomfort, especially the nose and eyes.

Approximate Size Comparison of a Cougar, Lynx, Bobcat, and Domestic Cat
[©2013 www.huffingtonpost.ca] [©2010 Keith Williams] [©2010 Bill W Ca] [photos-public-domain.com]

Cougar, Lynx, and Bobcat Safety

- Do not turn and run!
- Pick up small children (or pets) so they cannot panic and flee.
- MAINTAIN direct eye contact.
- Speak softly at first.
- BACK away slowly.

If the cougar doesn't leave, continue backing away and begin **loudly and firmly yelling at the cougar.** "Get-the-hell-outta-here, Cougar! Shoo! Go away!" Blowing a whistle is also effective.

Do all you can to appear larger. For example, open your jacket, raise and widely wave your arms, while continuing to loudly and firmly yell at the cougar. The goal is to convince the predator that you are a **danger** to it—*not* an easy meal.

If the cougar starts to follow you—something that rarely ever happens— **pick up sticks or stones and throw them at the cat as hard as you can.** Again, the goal is to demonstrate that you are not an easy meal.

Trees are *not* a means of escape. Cats are even more agile in trees than bears.

If attacked, fight back! Playing dead does *not* work with cougars.

Whack the attacking cat with anything you can reach—sticks, stones, or just your fists—aiming at its face. Kick at the cat's tender underbelly. Do *anything* you possibly can to cause discomfort.

Roosevelt Elk [©2013 Tara Miller]

Moose, Deer, and Elk Safety

- **Do not go near them, no matter how docile they appear.**
  If they feel threatened, moose, deer, and elk may strike at you with
  sharp hooves or antlers—or both. Since you'll not see a hidden deer
  fawn, moose or elk calf, you cannot anticipate what these animals
  might consider threatening. Do not go near them.
- **Do not feed them.** Feeding moose, deer or elk is harmful to the
  animal's health.
- **Shout and wave your arms.**
- **BACK away.**

Under most circumstances, moose, deer, and elk are easily frightened away.
If there's a calf or fawn hidden nearby, backing away also will demonstrate
that you're not threatening the baby.

Moose and deer are plentiful in all British Columbia wilderness areas.
Deer can even be encountered in urban areas.

Roosevelt Elk are often seen wandering through the *yards* of homes in
Forks and other small towns in the US Olympic Peninsula. In British Colum-
bia, however, the only place you're likely to encounter them is on Vancouver
Island.

http://en.wikipedia.org/wiki/Roosevelt_elk

[©2005 Darkone] [©2013 Dave Menke]

Raccoon Safety

- Yell or blow a whistle.
- Stamp your feet.
- Clap your hands and wave your arms.
- BACK away.

Thousands of incredibly cute, cuddly-looking raccoons range far and wide throughout the Olympic Peninsula and British Columbia. Normally timid and harmless, raccoons have razor sharp teeth and claws. Happily, as long as you don't corner and threaten one, it is unlikely that any raccoon will physically attack you.

British Columbia raccoons are not rabies carriers. The most common danger posed by human/raccoon contact is the threat of **becoming infected by the roundworm parasites frequently found in their feces**. The best way to avoid contracting roundworm is to stay away from raccoons and **watch where you step**. Since you probably won't know what kind of animal scat you're looking at, it's a good idea to simply **avoid stepping in *any* pile of pooh you encounter**.

Please Do Not Feed the Raccoons

When people feed them, raccoons lose their fear of humans and become accustomed to obtaining food from them. Next, they become more aggressive in their efforts to take food from humans. Although these masked bandits have never been known to attack people, raccoons may accidentally **bite or gouge** the digits that dangle a tasty tidbit.

http://en.wikipedia.org/wiki/Raccoon
http://www.spca.bc.ca/welfare/wildlife/urban-wildlife/raccoons.html

Stellar Sea Lions Elephant Seal Male, Female, and Pup
[©2006 Yummifruitbat] [©2009 Mike Baird]

Seals and Sea Lion Safety
Stay away from them!
It's as simple as that.

In British Columbia, it is unlawful as well as dangerous to approach a marine mammal any closer than 100 meters/yards (the length of an American football field)—even if the animal is *dead*.

Sea lions in particular are known to carry a potentially lethal bacterial disease called **leptospirosis**, which can be transferred to humans. Never touch a dead marine mammal.
http://en.wikipedia.org/wiki/Leptospirosis
http://www.cdc.gov/leptospirosis/

> "In humans, [Leptospirosis] can cause a wide range of symptoms, some of which may be mistaken for other diseases. Some infected persons, however, may have no symptoms at all. Without treatment, Leptospirosis can lead to kidney damage, meningitis (inflammation of the membrane around the brain and spinal cord), liver failure, respiratory distress, and even death."

If you see an injured, possibly sick, or stranded marine animal—or an incident of marine animal harassment—call the Department of Fisheries and Oceans Canada (DFO) hotline: **1-800-465-4336.**
http://www.pac.dfo-mpo.gc.ca/fm-gp/species-especes/mammals-mammiferes/report-signaler-eng.html

Northern Pacific Rattlesnakes
[©www.bib.ge/reptiles/open.php?id=1629] [©2006 StormTwin] [©2010 Cheryl Young]

Snake Safety

- Stay on the path or hiking trail.
  Never put your hands or feet where you cannot see them.
- Avoid disturbing logs and piles of rocks.
  If possible, walk *around* logs and rock piles rather than blindly stepping over them.
- **If you hear a rattlesnake, STOP MOVING immediately.**
  Pay attention to the sound and determine where the snake is hiding.
- **If you are close to the snake, REMAIN STILL.**
  Give the snake time to calm down and slither away.
- If the snake doesn't leave before your patience expires,
  slowly BACK away from it, go around it, and quickly leave the area.
- Do not poke or handle a snake.
- Never touch a dead rattlesnake.
  The biting reflex remains intact even after death.

British Columbia is home to nine species of snakes, only one of which is poisonous enough to threaten humans: the **Northern Pacific Rattlesnake**. (Photos above.)
http://bib.ge/reptiles/open.php?id=1629
https://wildsafebc.com/rattlesnake/

Happily, Northern Pacific Rattlesnakes—as well as their non-venomous look-alikes—prefer British Columbia's dry, south-central interior valleys. The Twilight Saga sites closest to rattlesnake habitat are about 100 miles (150 km) away: Jacob Black's house (Site #25), and Widgeon Slough Marsh, Coquitlam (Site #26). It would be incredibly unusual for you to encounter a rattlesnake at these sites.

BC rattlers have a triangular-shaped head and come in a variety of hues, based on the color of their environment: olive-green, gray, brown, golden, reddish brown, yellowish, or tan. The feature that most distinguishes them from similarly-colored, non-venomous snakes—like the **Great Basin Gopher Snake** and the **Night Snake**—is the rattle at the end of their tail.

Please Note: When feeling threatened, a gopher snake may mimic a rattlesnake's rattling noise by shaking and vibrating the end of its tail in leaves and dried vegetation. Apparently, gopher snakes are bright enough to recognize that they'll be safer if you think you're facing a rattlesnake. A very scared and threatened gopher snake may even coil like a rattler, hiss and strike out.

Great Basin Gopher Snake Night Snake
[©Gary Nafis] [©TigerQuoll]

Bottom Line: A snake encounter of any kind while Twilighting in British Columbia is not likely. In addition to snake bites being a rare occurrence, even rattlesnake bites are almost never fatal to humans. Snake bites that do occur are most often caused by people deliberately trying to handle or harm them. The most important thing to remember is to leave the snake alone!

If You are Bitten:

- Stay calm and move slowly.
- Remove any constrictive clothing or jewelry, which otherwise would act as a tourniquet—preventing fresh blood from entering the area (which is desirable), and concentrating the venom in one area (which is undesirable).
- If someone can carry you to the car park or nearest extraction point, that would be best. Otherwise, move slowly to an extraction point.
- Have someone drive you to the nearest hospital, or phone 911.
- Mark swelling with lines and times every 10 minutes or so. This will help doctors assess the severity of the bite.

DO NOT:

- Apply a tourniquet or ice.
- Make any incision over the bite or attempt to suck out the venom.
- Kill the snake and bring it to the hospital. Snakes are protected by law and doctors do not need to identify the snake to treat a snakebite.

To learn about the eight species of non-venomous British Columbia snakes, go to:
http://www.bcreptiles.ca/snakes.htm

Wolf and Coyote Red Fox, Coyote, Wolf
[©2008 Travis S] [©US National Park Service]

Wolf, Coyote, and Fox Safety

- If you happen upon an animal carcass of any kind, quickly leave the vicinity.
  Carrion (dead animals) constitutes a large portion of a wild canine's diet. Coastal wolves are particularly fond of dead fish and are frequently seen on Vancouver Island beaches.
- **Do not turn and run!**
- Pick up small children (or pets) so they cannot panic and flee.
- **MAINTAIN direct eye contact.**
- **BACK away slowly.**
- Make loud noises.
  Yell, blow a whistle, bang pots and pans together if you're camping.
- Do all you can to appear larger and threatening.
  Raise and widely wave your arms, open and flap the sides of your jacket. Throw rocks, sticks, sand—anything—at the predator.

Wolves, coyotes, and foxes are not normally a danger to humans, unless humans habituate them by providing them with food. The greater the space between people and wild canines, the safer it is for both of them. Never purposely get closer than 100 yards/meters (the length of an American football field), and never feed them.

Disclaimers

Novels as incredibly popular as Stephenie Meyer's *Twilight Saga* series inevitably generate an amazing number of **unauthorized** guides, companion books, philosophical essay collections, and the like. To avoid the threat of copyright or trademark infringement litigation, such unauthorized *Twilight Saga*-related books publish at least one **Disclaimer**. Below are **several Disclaimers** important *Tour the Twilight Saga* travel guidebooks.

This is an Unauthorized *Twilight Saga* Travel Guidebook

Tour the Twilight Saga Book Two [hereinafter referred to as **TTTS Two**] is not authorized, approved, endorsed, nor licensed by Stephenie Meyer; Summit Entertainment, LLC; Little, Brown and Company; Hachette Book Group, Inc.; Time Warner Book Group; nor by any other persons, entities, corporations or companies claiming a proprietary interest in the *Twilight Saga* books, movies, or related merchandise.

TTTS Two is not officially associated with the four *Twilight Saga* novels written and copyrighted by Stephenie Meyer. Nor is TTTS Two in any way officially associated with the five *Twilight Saga* movies produced and trademarked by Summit Entertainment.

The Purpose of Tour the Twilight Saga Book Two

TTTS Two was written solely for the purpose of providing an historical review of, and directions for finding, the real-world film sites located in and around Vancouver, British Columbia.

Twilight-Associated Names, Places, Titles or Terminology

TTTS Two does not claim, nor does it intend to imply, ownership of, or proprietary rights to, any of the character or place names, titles or terminology, used or created by Stephenie Meyer within her *Twilight Saga* novels, or the movies made thereof.

Publication of *Twilight Saga* Movie Screenshots

Screenshots (aka screen-caps) are split-second, still photographs captured when playing a movie on a computer. Several of the 14 Twilight Saga film site location chapters in TTTS Two—as well as the five inaccessible film sites in Chapter 16—include one or more movie or DVD Special Features screenshots.

The sole purpose of including these screenshots is to enhance the experience of *Twilight Saga* fans [**Twilighters**] while they visit these locations. By observing screenshots when onsite, Twilighters are reminded of what was seen on screen—even though special effects may have altered the real-world location's appearance.

To be an effective reminder of the movie locales, however, these screenshots had to be altered in a variety of ways, so that the film site's **background** can be more easily recognized. Some of them are screenshot *segments*—all of them are "enhanced" to improve the site's background recognition.

All five *Twilight Saga* movies were produced and trademarked by Summit Entertainment. TTTS Two does not claim, nor does it intend to imply, ownership of, or proprietary rights to, any portions of the *Twilight Saga* movies.

The caption of every screenshot that appears within TTTS Two should officially include the following copyright caveat: "™©Summit Entertainment, LLC." Inclusion of that information, however, would cause each screenshot's caption to be two lines long. Because this info is given *here*, we can save room by captioning screenshots only with identification of the movie (or DVD Special Features segment) from which each was captured.

Use of Google or Bing Maps Images

In order to assist Twilighters to find Twilight Saga film sites—especially within areas that include more than one filming location, such as the New Westminster and Gastown areas of Vancouver—we created a few **Vancouver, BC Twilight Saga Maps** for Book Two. We used segments of Google Maps images; cropped, enhanced, and married them; then added Twilight Saga site indicators. One Twilight Saga map was created with a Bing Map image. These maps are freely posted on our website.
http://www.TourTheTwilightSaga.com/B2/VBCtsMaps.pdf

Full-sized maps within the PDF contain appropriate attributions, crediting Google (or Bing/Microsoft) and contributing data providers. Below the thumbnail-sized Twilight Saga map images published in the travel guidebook, only Google or Bing is credited, so as to save space.

Within some chapters, we used segments of Google or Bing map images to illustrate a site's location, or segments of Google Street View images to demonstrate a site's most recent appearance.

ANH and TTTS do not claim, nor intend to imply, ownership of, or proprietary rights to, any of the Google Maps image segments—or Google Street view image segments—used within TTTS travel guidebooks or the supplemental PDFs posted on TourTheTwilightSaga.com.

ANH and TTTS do not claim, nor intend to imply, ownership of, or proprietary rights to, any of the Bing Maps image segments (©Microsoft Corporation) used within TTTS travel guidebooks or the supplemental PDFs posted on TourTheTwilightSaga.com.

Author vs Authors of *Tour the Twilight Saga*

The **A Novel Holiday** (ANH) travel guidebook publishing company concept was solely conceived by Ms. Charly D. Miller, as was the concept of the *Tour the Twilight Saga* travel guidebook series. During the researching and writing of TTTS travel guidebooks—as well as during TTTS website design—Ms. Miller was so generously assisted by other individuals, that she feels unworthy of claiming sole credit for authoring the texts' or websites' content. Thus, **plural terms**—such as, "authors" ... "we" ... "our"—are used throughout TTTS travel guidebooks and the website when referring to the writers or creators of same.

For all legal purposes, however, every A Novel Holiday *Tour the Twilight Saga* travel guidebook was solely written by CD Miller. She, alone, is responsible for all content published within any TTTS travel guidebook paperback, eBook, or PDF; as well as being solely responsible for all content posted on the ANH and TTTS websites.

Ms. Charly D Miller hereby avows and affirms that any and all other individuals who participated in or contributed to the researching, writing, or publication of *Tour the Twilight Saga* travel guidebooks and their associated websites, are **indemnified and held harmless** from and against: any and all demands, claims, and damages to persons or property, losses and liabilities, including attorney's fees arising out of or caused by any form of litigation brought against the A Novel Holiday *Tour the Twilight Saga* travel guidebooks or websites.

Credits and Acknowledgments

Tour the Twilight Saga Art

Two terrifically talented graphic artists designed our gorgeous Tour the Twilight Saga travel guidebook logo, and the three Twilight Saga Site Rating Icons: **Karen Dale** (neé Stoehr) and **Ben Dale**.

http://www.coroflot.com/dalek/profile
http://bendale.daportfolio.com/about

Tour the Twilight Saga Book Two Cover

DC Carson used a rights-managed image from Shutterstock to create the Twilicious cover of TTTS Book Two.

Photo Credits

If it is known, beneath each photograph in TTTS Book Two is a caption containing the name of the person who snapped the pic and the year in which it was taken. Some photos were obtained online from **Wikipedia** or **Wikimedia**, where they were posted by photographers who generously offered their commercial re-use freely.

A few photos, however, were obtained from Internet sites that neglected to provide photographer identification and contact information. If we've used *your photo* without asking permission, please Email us so we can request permission to continue using it, properly credit your photo, and properly thank you for letting us use it.
chas@novelholiday.com

Personal Acknowledgements from Author, CD Miller

Thank you, Tara!

Ms. Tara Miller of Findlay, Ohio—my *sister*, though not a blood relation!—is our most dedicated *Tour the Twilight Saga* travel guidebooks contributor. She voluntarily performed hundreds of Internet research hours, and helped to discover important Twilight Saga Sites that might otherwise have been missed. Tara also joined me on my September 2013 recon trip of Washington's Olympic Peninsula. Because she takes far better pix than I do, Tara's photography was a huge boon to TTTS Book One. I dearly wish she'd been with me in Vancouver!

Thank You, to All the Others Who Helped

The people listed below generously assisted with research and/or contributed photos to TTTS Book Two. Thank you for helping us ensure the accuracy of Book Two's content.

- Lee A. Wood
  http://www.leespage.ca/h/travel/canada/bc/sasamat_lake.html

- Nancy Tinari
  http://nancytinariedits.com/

- Douglas Cameron: a volunteer with the BC Entertainment Hall of Fame
  http://www.bcentertainmenthalloffame.com/

- 50 Shades Girl Portland (aka Twilight Girl Portland)
  http://50shadesgirlportland.com/ http://twilightgirlportland.com/

- Corinne Johnston of VanDusen Botanical Garden
  http://vandusengarden.org/

- Hayley Simpson
  http://www.hayleyonholiday.com/

- Karen Lee, Public Programs Manager for Gulf of Georgia Cannery
  http://gulfofgeorgiacannery.org
- Thomas McIlwraith
  http://www.anthroblog.tadmcilwraith.com/2010/04/30/sea-to-sky-cultural-journey/
- Gillian McMillan
  www.gillianmcmillan.com
- Jimmy Abbott
  www.onelifeonewhistler.com

My Biggest Thank You Goes to Ms. Dina C. Carson

I am more grateful to DC Carson than mere words can possibly convey.

Dina has helped with all my ANH travel guidebook projects from the very beginning—back in 2007. She nursed me through the writing of my first series, the five *Harry Potter Places* travel guidebooks. And now she's helping me with *Tour the Twilight Saga*. Without Dina's astute writing guidance and editing talents, ANH travel guidebooks would be *awful*.

My fondest wish is to someday be able to reciprocate by helping Dina in some manner. Unfortunately, because she is far more talented than I am at *everything*, it is unlikely that I'll ever be able to do as much work for her as she's done for me. Hopefully, however, I'll someday be able to financially reward her.

To learn about the many marvelous books Dina has written, visit her Iron Gate Publishing website:

http://www.irongate.com

Thank you, Thank you, Thank you, Dahlink Dina!

To My Personal Friends:

Susan and Bob, Jamie, Janet and Mike, Chet, Leeenda and Mike, the Greene Sibdiblings ... these are just a few of the *scores* of people I have to thank! Each of these individuals have contributed—in their own way—to ensuring that I can continue pursuing my ANH travel guidebook projects. You guys have no idea how much I appreciate your help, and how much I value your friendship.

Lastly, to Drew and Annabeth, Auntie Dot and Uncle Itchy:

Bless You for always believing in me.

Index

The End

Thus ends the adventures of tour the twilight saga book two. Please join us in oregon and washington for book three.

CPSIA information can be obtained
at www.ICGtesting.com
Printed in the USA
LVHW052350011221
705049LV00036B/391

9 781938 285233